To truly exist is knowing that
nothing is ever perfect.

Synopsis

Kensie Newman found love at an early age. She spent every summer in Florida with her grandmother and her best friend, Gabriel Jack. She knew he forever held her heart. She envisioned the two of them would never be separated. When her grandmother passes away, she loses contact with Gabriel. As she grows older, none of her relationships seem to mean as much to her as the one she shared with Gabriel. As she moves on with her life, and fifteen years later, she's had several ex-boyfriends, a failed marriage, and two children. She suddenly finds herself rekindling her friendship with Gabriel. She tries to put the past behind her to see what happens, but she never forgot every moment they spent together. Wanting to tell him she never let him go, wanting to tell him how much she always loved him, while trying to remember she is an adult now. As she dives into a blast from the past, something unexpected happens. It's a ride she fought her whole life to get on; and one that took a turn in the right direction. For the hopeless romantic, for anyone that's ever lost a love or rekindled an old flame, everything truly does happen for a reason.

Dedication

To my mother, **Brenda Jean Downs**; with whom I never shared the gift of love with until God almost took you from me. We've had our share of disagreements and I've made many mistakes-but I still love you mom, I couldn't have made it here without you.

…and to my father, **Ronald Ray Downs**, I wish you were here to read this; you truly helped me be who I am today. Your passing changed me forever but also helped me live by this motto:

'What feeds the soul-
Never leaves the soul.'

Author's Note

I was an inexperienced college freshman when bits and pieces of Irony were started. I used the knowledge I gained during my college career to complete this book. The beginning and the ending were changed (on several occasions) while supporting my family through work and college. As my writing experience grew, I learned new ways to create characters and make their lives realistic. I owe a plethora of gratitude and give a multitude of respect to my professors who helped me learn while attending IU East. My message is not to give up; struggles are there to make you appreciate everything that lies at the end of the road. Being given something means nothing, until you work for what you want, the satisfaction becomes reality.

The dream of a young girl to write a book one day has been succeeded. I told my dad when I was ten I was going to write a book someday. He told me I wouldn't and that I needed to follow a business career path because he wanted me to have more than he ever did. I still wrote, I never forgot about my dream of writing a book and after five years in the making, when I got my proof, he's the first person I wanted. I did not want to rub it in his face, I wanted to tell him that I didn't write it to get rich, I wrote it to tell a story.

I would like to thank Sarah Grubbs for helping me gather the information I needed about Santa Monica to write this book, Dana Dean for creating my cover-you are amazing, maybe we will get the next one to fit right! Chris Reed for fixing the DPI on my author photo and my cover picture-I learned a lot from this experience! Sandra Strange for doing my professional pictures, and everyone who read the rough drafts that led to the final outcome. I cannot begin to name everyone who took an interest in this book, or begin to thank everyone who supported me emotionally while I fought and struggled for perfection. Heather, Kelsey, Brenda, Amber, Jacob, Misty, you guys read thru this mess and I want to thank you. When I got my proof, and realized some changes needed to be made, my friend Beth looked at me and said, "It isn't ever going to be good enough for you, it will have its flaws, it's like a child, you learn from your mistakes." She was right. I looked at my digital proof over and over, then searched my hand held proof and realized it wasn't perfect and that's not what life was about. There are mistakes and I'm leaving them there, because they reflect my ability to grow and it gives me something to nurture. The first few chapters are a bit rushed, but I left myself open to a future book or prequel.

To Seth, as some of the ironic parts of this book are in my life now, unknowing when written, given when I was least expecting it. Most of all to music-for the inspirational points that started pieces of this book…without music in the world, creativity would be lost.

To my boys, **Malachi**, **Gage**, and **Noah**; thank you for keeping me on my toes. There's never a dull moment. I may not agree with the things you say or do, as you grow older, not a single day goes by that I do not love you. For that, do what makes you happy, because at the end of the day, when you look in the mirror, it's only yourselves you have to answer to.

IRONY

Chapter Contents

Chapter 1-My Epic Love

It was a normal September morning when my mother told me we were driving to Sarasota. "Why?" I asked her because this was different than my normal routine. My grandma lived there and I looked forward to staying with her in the summers, two months out of every year from the age of four until I was fifteen. I had just come back from Florida the month before and didn't really understand why we were making a mid-fall trip back.

My parents never said a word to me; or to each other the entire trip there. I just shut my eyes and drifted into a day dream. *At least I get to see Gabriel again this summer* is all I thought about. When I woke up from time to time, my mother would just turn around and smile with a sad look on her face. She waited until we got there to tell me my grandmother had passed away so it would seem real to me.

"My grandma is not gone." I told my mother as we stood outside my grandmother's house. "She can't be; she can't leave me like this." I proceeded to say with huge tears running out of my eyes. My mother grabbed my hands lightly and tried to give me a hug. I broke away from her and stood there in my own desperation. I didn't want her to console me; I wanted her to make it go away.

My grandmother was the greatest person I knew; she was the one person who always understood me. My mom looked like her, and I loved my mom, but my grandma was the only person who eventually let me be me. She never raised her voice, she never punished me for the gazillion things I did wrong; she had this beautiful smile, wore her flowered dresses, and always had her hair in a poodle perm. She used to let me drink soda and coffee on the back dock early in the day.

She used to brush my long, frizzy brown hair and put it in braids. She taught me how to cook and bake and on my fourteenth birthday, she taught me how to wear makeup and how certain colors accented my light brown eyes. She would say, "Only light colors, nothing dark, it isn't proper for a young girl to wear a lot of makeup." That was the year she gave me her gold wedding band. My dad bought me a bracelet to match it some years later; I wore it on my right hand. She always made me wear more clothing, even though it was summer, and she never let me wear a two piece bathing suit.

She used to sit me down every visit and tell me lady's don't climb trees and ride skateboards. She said I needed to start acting like a lady because one day, some boy would ask me to marry him and it would be an infinite bond. I always thought it was the boy next door, Gabriel Jack.

"But grandma, Gabriel climbs trees and rides a bike, and I want to play with him." I said to her at the age of eight.

"Someday Gabriel isn't going to want to hang out with you Kensie, you need to find some little girls to play dolls with." She said back as she smiled, handing me flowers to put in a vase.

"He wants to play with me, I promise he does, he won't play dolls." I said back to dispute her argument. She would make her remarks and then finally give up and tell me to go outside. She wasn't one to argue.

Once when I was ten, she sat Gabriel and I down and made him play dolls with me, he was so mad, he took the boy doll outside and tied him to a tree. She finally gave up trying to get me to be a girl; it wasn't until I was twelve that I actually wore a dress. She tried so hard to keep Gabriel and me apart, but she couldn't do much about it, we were inseparable. She would come outside, see us playing and shake her head as she pulled up weeds or planted flowers.

Suddenly all this came back to me as I stood there looking at the yard. It hit me like a ton of bricks; it was the worst pain I had to endure. I didn't care that my mother was grieving her loss, it wasn't about her; it was about me-my whole life was about to change, and I knew it.

My grandfather had passed away when I was five, it was the first time I had experienced death, but I didn't really remember it. I looked at all the people coming in and going out of my grandmother's once quiet little house.

She had been fine all summer; she didn't complain of anything my whole trip, a month later, she was gone. My mother tried to explain her kidneys had failed, *what happened to her kidneys* was the only thing I could think about. *She was fine, she was fine.* I just kept telling myself that this was a joke. All I could do was run, fast, and far away. Far away to me was the back yard. I imagine my mom left me alone because she knew Gabriel would follow me. I ran so fast to the dock that I tripped over a board, fell, and skinned my knees.

I might have been crying harder because of the blood running down my legs, but I didn't really care, I ran with the boys, I climbed trees like a boy, but for some reason, I cried like a girl. The hurt of life was the worst pain of all.

Gabriel stood above me with his hands in his pockets for hours and listened to me cry. I was so exhausted that I laid down on the dock-face down-so I could see the water through the boards; I watched my tears fall as they rolled off my face like rocks pinging against the water. Gabriel sat down next to me, reached over and grabbed my hand, pulling me towards him. I leaned on his chest and cried so hard that I soaked his shirt; I listened to his heart beat for what seemed like forever.

Gabriel kissed me on the forehead; then moved to my nose, a subtle kiss on my mouth was followed by a deep, long, loving kiss, and he told me everything would be okay. I told him it wouldn't, that I would probably never see him again; he promised me that I would, but I didn't believe him. That first kiss with a boy didn't last long and it was the last time I talked to him, I tried to write him several times, but couldn't find it in myself to send it out. I never received one letter or phone call from him, I often look back now and think maybe my parents had something to do with that, like maybe he did and they didn't tell me, or maybe, just maybe…he felt like I did.

I did some therapy after that, my therapist told me I needed some closure, I cried every day, I don't know if I cried because of my grandma, or because of Gabriel, but I know being a teenager was hard enough. That didn't make it any better.

Gabriel Jack and I lost our friendship in the sands of time, I had never found another friend who I admired, respected, and longed to love like him. My mother used to tease me; she would say, "Kensie, you two are going to get married someday." After my grandmother died, I never went back to Florida. My impression of guys somewhat diminished because I based my relationships on the one I had with Gabriel. He was the sweetest boy I had ever met; maybe I fell in love with him because, well, he was-my best friend.

When we weren't fishing, we were making up stories and writing it down in books that I still have. When we grew older, we rode bikes a lot. His bike was a dirt bike, and he always beat me but I never got tired of chasing him. We climbed trees, played cards, and got into a lot of trouble.

An epic love to me was the feeling I had when I shared a breath with Gabriel-after running down the beach, or through someone's back yard, laying on the dock behind my grandma's house telling jokes and my silly laugh; watching him play basketball in his driveway with his long shorts and tank top…he always wore a New York Yankee's cap turned backwards…the same Yankee's cap the entire time I knew him. Every summer I went to visit my grandmother, I noticed the difference in his growth, but I never paid much attention to it because my love for him never changed.

Every time he touched me, I melted. When I was not visiting my grandma, we would write back and forth, or call when our parents would let us. I might have been young, too young some people would have said, to really know the meaning of love, but when you know it; and feel it, you can't deny it.

We held hands on occasion as we grew older, but he never kissed me until…my grandma died. I have thought about him often throughout the years. *What has he been doing? Is he married? Does he have kids? What's he look like?* I just wanted to see a picture of him. Often people you had crushes on when you were a kid do not look anything like you would expect them to look as you grow older. I never found any one quite like him; I never let anyone get that close to me-not even my ex-husband.

To this day, I dream about a guy; who never has a face, he haunts me from time to time. It's almost like I'm looking for him, sometimes I see him; sometimes I'm trying to make him notice me. It's the same dream, over and over. It has to be Gabriel. Maybe my mind just won't let it go and my sub conscious takes over when I'm sleeping. I have to believe that someday, somehow, he's out there. I just haven't found him yet.

Sure; I have met some nice guys along the way, there's Roy, the boy my father tried to set me up with who worked at the grocery store. He ended up going to college in Texas. The neighbor boy, Jason, who I thought was so hot but he never really noticed me no matter how hard I tried. Once I even wore my bathing suit out to get the mail and all he did was smile and wave. I found out later that he didn't like girls at all-I guess that explained some of it.

Once I was at the school library and Jared, the boy with dreamy deep blue eyes, came over-sat next to me, and asked me for my phone number. He called me a few times then fell off the face of the earth. I met Tim when I was 21 and worked at a retail store. He had sandy blond hair and a beautiful smile. We used to lay in my parent's back yard and watch the stars, he was really smart, knew everything about the cosmos, but he broke it off about 6 months later and I was heartbroken.

Brian was the guy I met later on that year and he used me for every penny I made. I gave him whatever he wanted. No, I wasn't rich, but I handled my finances well. I knew he was using me and one day, I got tired of it and told him I was done.

I gave up on dating for a while and focused on work and helped my friend Nora on her ranch. A year later I met someone who helped her dad train horses and we had a great relationship. He reminded me of Gabriel, blond hair and deep blue eyes but then one day he just stopped talking to me.

I dated Dan from the next town over the year before I got married. I truly loved his freckled face and his 6'3 stature but for some reason, he just didn't think like I did. I always thought about my future and he didn't really place me in his. He would come and go, break up, then call me and I finally told him a few months later that I wasn't that girl.

I met Clay when I started working for a small ad agency, he was a starving artist, and not long after we met, I got pregnant, and it never really seemed right. Throughout the years and two girls later, I never felt complete. None of my relationships seemed to have the right timing. I simply gave up on finding the love I desired. Thru every wrong turn I made, and a ridiculously long divorce, in the back of my mind, I never really forgot Gabriel.

Chapter 2-Remember Me?

Fifteen years later I was almost thirty-one and the single mother of two daughters, Rayanne, eight, and Marie, five. Although my feelings towards the epic love I desired were put on hold, I returned to school to get a degree in Journalism. I always wanted to write, that was another thing Gabriel and I had in common.

In the creative world of the internet, I was thumbing through a social network site one day while I was on my lunch break at work. While eating some chips and drinking a soda, I seen his name come across my screen. The picture looked like the same boy I knew, only older. I could tell it was him because of his eyes. After almost spitting out my soda, I sat staring out into the huge city for a while.

My heart was bouncing around in my chest; I could feel it. My hands were shaking, my palms sweating. I watched the same cloud move from one side of the sky to the next. *It couldn't be, could it?* I wasn't the same young girl anymore, I had babies to take care of, I had no time to be chasing crazy dreams…before I knew it; I had sent him a friend request with a message asking if he remembered me.

I checked that web site every day for days; every time I logged on, I was nervous. Nothing. The days passed, and I was beginning to wish I hadn't sent it. Maybe he didn't remember me at all.

I stopped checking it after a few months; I tried to put it out of my head. I refrained from looking at his private page since I couldn't see much of it anyway. I would change my pictures every so often and know that my picture would show up on his friend request. I tried to find pictures of me that were beautiful and I once added a picture of us knowing he might see it one day and think about our past. I finally gave up and avoided the website for a few months. I was heartbroken, again, and he hadn't even done anything. I was too proud to tell anyone I found him, too embarrassed to tell anyone I sent that and he didn't reply.

Eventually I logged back on, although I didn't forget about it, I didn't expect anything. He had accepted my friend request a few weeks earlier and sent a message back that said, "Hell yeah, I remember you!" For about six months we emailed back and forth. We exchanged phone numbers but I thought at the time if he wanted to call, he would, I never attempted to call him. I guess I was still a bit shy; I never really grew out of that.

I never told my parents or anyone else that we were communicating because I knew they would think I was crazy. My mom knew what I had gone through with my grandma's death, and loosing Gabriel as my best friend. She was the one who sat with me in therapy when I was sixteen, and it took a long time for me to dissolve that life from reality. I didn't want her to know I had slipped back into the fairy tale. Nora, who had been my best "girl" friend since we were five, didn't even know I had found him. She knew all about him, but I didn't want her to make a big deal out of it so I never said a word.

Gabriel and I had a pretty normal internet relationship; but it was almost like meeting someone new online. We emailed a lot because he wasn't on that social site very often. I wanted to tell Nora about it, but I was afraid to. I was afraid of everything. One day I decided to take a long lunch and called Nora to see if she wanted to go. We met me at a little restaurant not far from my office building.

I finally decided to tell her my news; it had been eating at me for a while.

"I found Gabriel." I said as we sat down.

"Excuse me?" She said back as she leaned her head in. She didn't have a very approving look on her face.

"I found Gabriel. We have been emailing back and forth for a while now." I said calmly.

"So, the next thing you say…will be to explain to me why you didn't tell me?" She said with a still look on her face.

"It's not like I was looking for him." I said sitting back in my chair.

I knew this wasn't going to be a good conversation. The waiter came over to bring us our drinks and we ordered the same thing we always get. Nora was beautiful, with dark eyes, dark perfect hair, outgoing, and miserable in her own relationship. She had been dating the same guy for the last eight years, they had no children, but she refused to get married.

She had owned horses for as long as I could remember, she didn't want or need anything. Her family had a lot of money, and she hated anything or anyone that might become happy because she said nothing lasts forever and at some point they become miserable. Poor girl. I told her once she just had to have a little faith in love. She came back with some smart comment about practicing what I preach and I informed her that I just put that on hold. We sat in silence for a few minutes, I just started looking around the restaurant; I knew she was staring at me but I couldn't look her in the eyes.

"So, how does he look?" Nora sat back and finally smiled, "Is he still as cute as he was when he was younger?" She asked as she took a drink of her soda. I just sat there…

"Well?" She asked again.

"He's gorgeous; he looks the same, just older-same baby blue eyes." I said calmly as I smiled.

"Well, you found him, stir up any feelings?" She said as she smiled.

She caved, I didn't think it would happen that quickly, but she looked like she might actually be interested in letting me be happy for a minute.

"It makes me melt every time he writes me. I know we aren't kids anymore, we are grown adults. I know I have had a hard time getting over it, maybe I never did, but I am thankful that for once, only once, destiny took control." I said in one breathe with a dreamy smile.

"Here we go…" Nora said with a blank look on her face. I just sat there. "What does he do?" She asked as she smiled and put both her elbows on the table while pressing her face into her knuckles.

"I am not sure really, he said he works for a production company in Los Angeles, he owns a small club in Santa Monica, and…he has a son, Ethan, who is six." I said quietly.

"Is he married?" Nora leaned back in her chair and crossed her arms in disproval.

"Nope, he never got married." I offered.

"What do you guys talk about, I mean, I'll let the negative points of the situation go and focus on the good." Nora said with her mouth full.

"Why can't you just be happy for me, I'm happy, I don't want to talk about the negative outcome. I'm not a kid anymore; I know I can handle my own rejection. It's not like I haven't been through it before." I said sneering at her.

"You keep saying you aren't a kid anymore, but you rely on feelings that only exist in the mind of a fifteen year old girl." She said as she paused when she seen the horror on my face. "Okay, okay, I admit, it's crazy, you find him what, some fifteen years later, he isn't married, you are recently divorced, you have leaned on that relationship your entire life, it couldn't be any healthier." She snapped as she finished her lunch.

I hadn't touched mine. I was mad that she couldn't just be happy that I was happy. I know she was there when I went through it, yeah, yeah, I get it, but this is why I didn't tell her.

"This is why I didn't tell you." I said back with a frown on my face.

"Alright, give me the story, I'm listening." She said with disgust because she knew that she had to let me win, once.

"There isn't one, we just email back and forth." I said as I suddenly had no desire to talk about it anymore.

"So, what do you talk about? Do you still have feelings for him?" Nora said making a big deal out of it, just like I said she would.

"We just talk about whatever really, mostly about day to day things; sometimes we talk about things we recall from our pasts." I said quickly.

"Do you plan on seeing him? Like, in person?" She asked.

"Hum, well, since he lives in California and I live in Tennessee and I can't just go there and I don't see him just coming here, I am going to say NO." I said back sarcastically.

"I don't want to see you get hurt, Kensie, that's all I'm saying, but you never know, it might actually be meant to happen this way." She said as we got up from the table.

"Now that sounds like something my mother would say Nora; which is exactly why I haven't told her about it." I said sharply.

"YOU haven't told your mom yet?" Nora yelled.

"It's not that big of a deal." I said as I rolled my eyes.

"I think it is, and I think that you will meet him again, I have a feeling about this, not sure if it's good or bad, but I have a feeling." Nora said handing me my box of food I never touched.

"I don't know, my impression of guys is on the chopping block right now but… it feels great to check my email every second I get, butterflies in my stomach all over again. That's epic love, butterflies that never go away no matter how long you have been together." I said as I paid the bill.

"You should be happy more often; I get lunch bought for me." Nora said as she rolled her eyes.

"There is nothing you can say to me that I haven't said once or twice; or haven't heard before Nora." I said as I snapped back. We both loved to get one up on the other one and our sarcastic natures kept our friendship going as long as it had.

I think the problem with people is they have no hope, no expectation for love. It's not my fault that Nora was miserable in her relationship, I wasn't looking for anything out of Gabriel, maybe people need to realize that the universe speaks to us, and sometimes, we have to listen to it. Faith, we all just need a little bit of it from time to time. My thoughts might be unorthodox, I feel like everyone should be happy no matter what they do and the second they are not, they should let go of what is making them unhappy and be honest; after all, we lead one life and we have to make the best of it. It all comes down to faith; faith in what we want and what we believe.

I was really tired of hiding how I felt, maybe my haunting memory of Gabriel was a bit psychotic, but I couldn't change what I knew, or how I felt. I walked back to my office in a foul mood, I was hoping she would be a little bit more receptive of something that made me happy, and it wasn't even physical.

Chapter 3-The Meeting

For two years prior to rekindling my broken relationship with Gabriel, I had been taking four classes at a local community college and working full time for an ad agency in Nashville. I loved my job, but I really wanted my journalism degree. I eventually wanted to move to New York and get a job writing for a huge newspaper. Once the girls were grown, I could actually live my dream.

I had been checking my email for a few weeks since my lunch with Nora and I still had not received anything from Gabriel. I began to understand why she didn't want me to be disappointed, but I didn't let it affect me. I refrained from sending duplicate messages, and I tried really hard to put it out of my mind.

I did my same routine for the next couple of weeks, went to work, left work, did homework for my on-line classes, went home to spend time with my girls-then got up to do it all over again. No excitement. Nora and I hung out a few times, when she brought it up, I just changed the subject. I told her I was done talking about it. Her response never really left my mind: "That was short lived." Part of me was angry she even allowed herself to say that. My response: "You should see a doctor about medically inserting a filter in between your brain and mouth."

On the following Thursday; I was in the middle of my daily routine. I went into the main hall at about 3:00 to check on clients; there were five guys sitting in the waiting room.

Around there someone always knew some famous person and was looking for media advertising for someone else. One of the guys was a lot bigger than the rest, *what an entourage,* I thought to myself. Two of the guys had on baseball caps and sunglasses and the other three were dressed in business suits

I had on my blue business suit and heels, my hair was in a bun, I smiled and went on about my business. The receptionist told me the guys in the waiting room wanted to know if they could get a meeting with me and asked for me by name. They didn't look like people interested in southern advertising to me, but I went over and introduced myself anyway.

"Hello." I said as I normally did upon meeting new people.

"Hello, my name is Spencer Harrington and I am working with someone who is interested in hiring your company to advertise a movie being filmed here." He said as he stood up and shook my hand. He had a beautiful smile. When he shook my hand, he shocked me. Static electricity had built up and he shocked me! His hands were kind of soft but he had a strong grip.

"Nice to meet you, I'm Kensie Newman, sorry about that." I responded as I let go of his hand.

"It might have been me." He laughed as he shook his hand into the air. "I was wondering if you had time today to speak with me about a media presentation." He asked and said.

"I'm afraid I don't have an open appointment today, but I would love to schedule an appointment for you to come in with exact dates and what you are looking for." I said back smiling.

"I know that extras will be needed for filming and we would like to hire some locals for the positions. I was hoping your company could create an ad for us to get people interested in the film." Spencer said smiling back.

"Well, if you'd like to call me, I will give you my personal number," I said as I searched through my notebook for a business card, "I don't seem to have one with me, I'm sorry." I said.

"I can leave my card with you, if you would like, and maybe you could call me tomorrow to set up an appointment." He said reaching into his wallet to get his card out.

"That would be great, let me grab you a brochure so you know what we offer." I said taking the card and looking down to read it. I walked over to the receptionist's desk, grabbed a brochure, and as I turned around-they all were staring at me.

"Here you go; the number is on the back." I said as I nervously handed him the brochure.

"Thank you." Spencer said as he smiled. "Look forward to speaking with you again." He finished.

None of the guys spoke except Spencer, they just smiled and shook my hand but no one else said anything. I guess some people let other people do the talking for them. I kind of felt like they were up to something, either they were smiling because I had something on my face, or they were just being goofy, but they didn't stop smiling, especially Spencer.

I stood at the receptionist's desk and we both watched them walk out. She looked up at me and waved a paper across her face to fan herself.

"Hot." She smiled and said.

"Yeah, no kidding." I said as they left the office. "Do I have something on my face?" I said quickly and big eyed.

"No, I don't see anything. I'd like to give them a few minutes of my time." She said as she laughed.

"I wish I had a few to give them." I laughed and walked into my office.

About twenty minutes after I got back into my office, the receptionist rang me and said that I was wanted at the main door to our building. I thought it was Clay because I had been avoiding him for the last few months. We had a really bad divorce and I had no desire to talk to him. He hadn't even seen the girls in the last four months because he could never seem to pick them up on time.

Everything seemed to be an excuse or argument. If he had a tiny bit of sense in his little finger, we could get along enough for our girls. I wasn't scared, but it wasn't something I was looking forward to. I waited a few minutes, called her back and asked that she find out who it was.

She called me back to tell me that the receptionist at the main desk had no idea who it was and he did not give them a name. I got in the elevator and went down to the ground floor anticipating the worse; but it wasn't my ex-husband at all, it was Spencer, the guy I had just been talking to.

I thought to myself how adorable he was with his sunglasses now on top of his baseball cap, but people normally didn't ask me to come down to the main hall. It made me a bit nervous.

"Hello, again, I know this is a bit unorthodox, but someone wants to speak with you, outside." Spencer said.

"Who is it?" I asked in a confused voice looking out the windows.

"Gabriel Jack." Spencer said calmly.

"Gabriel Jack is here?" I exclaimed.

"Yeah, you could say that." Spencer laughed with his bright enticing hazel eyes.

Spencer was pretty tall, I'd guess about 6'4, at least he seemed really tall to me, and he would against my short 5'6 self. He didn't really have a baby face, but he looked young, he had side burns and a bit of stubble on his chin. He was pretty hot. He had on long jean shorts, black tennis shoes, black socks, and a tee shirt, yes, I was checking him out, it was hard not to. So I followed Spencer outside to the group of guys standing by a car in front of my office building. I stayed back a few feet until I heard a quiet voice say...

"Kensie Newman?"

"Gabriel Jack?" I asked.

"You didn't even recognize me!" He said laughing as he turned his hat backwards.

I walked closer to him. "You look, the same, but different! I see some things never change" I said as I smacked the side of his hat. "WHAT are you doing in Nashville?"

"Surprise!" Gabriel said as he held out his hands for a hug with a huge smile.

He had grown tremendously; he was about 6'1 and weighed about 180. He had on a tee shirt and some baggy shorts. His blond hair was short and his bangs were perfectly even sticking out in the front; or the back should I say, of his hat.

"I am definitely surprised! I wondered why you didn't email me back." I said as I hugged him closely.

He smelled so good, like a guy should, I couldn't quite make out the scent, but I had smelled it before. He was tan, I touched his stomach and his chest was hard as a rock. He must work out; his arms were of decent size, and muscular. I did not want to let go.

Gabriel released me from the hug but kept a hold of my hands. I was so nervous that they began to sweat. I could see a tribal art tattoo peeking out from the upper part of his right arm; I couldn't quit looking into his baby blue eyes. He didn't have any facial hair, but he had two diamond earrings in his left ear. He carried himself well. He still looked like the same athletic boy I remembered.

"I really did come to find out about your company, and I wanted to check you out first." Gabriel laughed and continued… "In which you do look great by the way, and I thought I would invite you to Santa Monica. We are in route to Florida for a meeting and heading back home. Gabriel paused and pointed, "You've met Spencer, that's Liam, Josh, and Nathan." Gabriel let go of my hands so I could officially shake theirs.

"Nice to meet you guys, Santa Monica, when?" I asked as I shook their hands. I wanted to release my long hair from the bun it was in to give my hands something to do but I decided not to.

"Next week, I know it isn't much time but after all this emailing back and forth, and the stress you sounded like you were under at work, I thought you could use the break." Gabriel firmly stated. "Plus, I wanted to see you." He finished.

"I totally told you I was going to take a vacation soon, you little jerk," I said as I playfully pushed him.

"I'm a jerk now, eh?" He said laughing and put his hand on my shoulder.

"You know what I mean; I did not expect you to just pop in ask me to fly across the United States to hang out with you!" I said as I started to feel my hands shake a little bit.

"Well, it's paid for so expect the unexpected. If we had more time, I'd take you out to dinner later but we really have to get going." Gabriel said with the most sincerity.

"What do you mean it's paid for?" I asked.

"I got the ticket for you; all you have to do is go to the airport and of course, pack your bags." Gabriel laughed as he took off his hat and replaced it back on his head.

"Wow, I don't know what to say, but thank you?" I said sounding like I was asking a question.

"Your welcome Kensie, email me later and let me know what your plan is and I will get back with you tomorrow; or, hey, just call me, don't email me, just call in the morning, do you still have the number?" Gabriel asked.

"Yes, I still have it." I said with a smile.

"Good, give me a hug, I gotta go." Gabriel held out his hands.

I asked myself, *is he touching me again? I can't believe he is touching me again.*

I gave Gabriel another hug, one that had been coming for a very long many years and although he had to go, I didn't want him to. I felt like it took me so long to find him, I didn't want to let go. It was butterflies all over again.

As soon as I turned to walk away, I wanted to turn around to see them drive off, but I didn't want to seem too excited, I didn't want him to think I was crazy, but I know I was smiling.

As soon as I opened the main door to my building, the receptionist came running up to me…

"I felt like I had to poke outside and make sure you were safe, I know you have had some issues with your ex and I apologize for intruding, but DO YOU KNOW WHO THAT WAS?" She said with excitement.

"Umm, yeah, an old friend of mine, I didn't even recognize him." I said with a half lit smile.

"That was Gabriel Jack, he is a producer, he was here, right here in this office!" She said as her face lit up with excitement.

"Are you sure about that? I think he just works for a production company." I said confused.

"No, I am positive he is a producer. He produces a sitcom I watch every week, and I saw him in a magazine promoting his new movie; it was an interview; there was a picture of him and the bigger guy that was standing out there. I know for a fact it was him." She said without taking a breath and put her hands on her hips.

She was more excited than I was but I thought she might have made an honest mistake. When I got back to my office, I used a search engine to find his name, and sure enough, she was right.

I began wondering if I had searched his name a long time ago what would have happened. I wondered if I might not have taken a journey to California just to see if I could run into him. There was nothing about his personal life on the internet, just a few movies and that sitcom he produced. He must have an awesome PR person. There were lots of pictures of him with Liam and some with Spencer.

Now I was really nervous. No wonder he had on sunglasses and a hat. I guess not only did he conceal his identity to me, but to most everyone around me but the main receptionist. I had never heard his name, ever, and I would have definitely remembered if I had. I knew lots of directors, but not many producers. I sat in my chair turning Spencer's card over and over, I couldn't help but smile because Gabriel was actually here.

I called Nora and then my mother. I was so excited that I couldn't talk right. I shortly explained to my mom how we had been emailing back and forth and that he was in Nashville. She took it better than I thought but the first thing out of her mouth was to yell at me for not telling her when I found him. Suddenly I felt like WE were yelling back and forth about how I didn't want everyone to think I was crazy. My mother was a tall woman with black hair and black eyes and when she was mad you knew it. She was loud-unlike my grandma; and she loved to have a good fight with my dad.

"See, I told you it was meant to be! I told you long ago if it were meant to be, it would be." My mother finally said after she stopped yelling at me.

"WHY does everyone keep saying that?" Although I knew my mother and Nora were the only ones who said that, it felt to me like that was everyone, I continued, "Nothing is really MEANT to be, it just means that 'I' am going to have a wonderful vacation, one that I need." I said back stressing the "I" part of the sentence.

"Oh honey, don't worry about anything, your dad and I will take care of the girls, and feed Cairo, and check the mail, and…" my mother tried to continue on…

"Mom, I will not be gone that long, but thank you for being willing to check the mail." I quickly changed the subject to more about Gabriel. "Do you know he produces his own work? Did you know he ended up being a producer? How have I never heard of him? What in the world am I going to talk to him about? I have nothing to offer him." My mother quickly cut me off.

"I'm sure he is the same person he always was, after all, he did come here to see you, don't analyze it Kensie; just go with it." My mother gave me her most mothering words.

"I know mom, I know. I can't help but to analyze things, it's a problem of mine." I said with discouragement. "What about Cairo? He will go nuts if he is left there for a week by himself!" I exclaimed.

Cairo was my Alaskan Husky who was almost 3 years old. He went everywhere with me. He slept with me; sat with me, we jogged together; he was just a big baby. That dog became my comforter when Clay and I broke up. I would have been lost without him, and I hadn't been without him since I got him.

"He will be fine, your dad can bring him over to our house and he can stay in the garage, he will be comfortable there, he can't tear anything up, it will be fine Kensie." My mother said trying to console my deepest thoughts.

The first thing I did when I got off the phone with her was leave work. I cancelled my appointments, probably not the most responsible thing to do, but I was excited. I jumped in my car and put in my love cd, music is my life, and drove off to buy batteries for my digital camera. I had to take lots of pictures-for my girls, yeah, for my girls.

I met Nora for dinner and we went shopping. I listened to her scold me about not getting my hopes up but I needed to buy this outfit and that outfit and shirts that showed off my chest.

"Get this dress…" She said. "It shows off your chest." She finished.

"Yeah, all 34 C of it." I laughed.

"That's what you need, something that pushes them right up there!" She said as she handed the dress to the sales lady.

"I can't afford that dress." I calmly told her as I took the dress back from the counter and put the hanger back on it.

"You can too, just take it out of your savings account. This doesn't happen all the time Kensie; I'll buy it for you." She said giving the dress back to the sales lady.

Needless to say, I bought the dress. I didn't even really like it. I didn't wear flowers very well. After we finished shopping, I went to pick up my girls from my parent's and my dad just kept smiling at me. He never said a word, just smiled. I grabbed the girls and ran because I didn't want to hear anything from my mother.

When I got home, I got up the courage to call him. It only took me about two hours. I waited until I put the girls in bed so I didn't have any interruptions. When he answered, I really didn't recognize his voice, it sounded so mature, so deep. He sounded happy to hear from me.

"Glad you called, didn't know if you would" Gabriel laughed.

"Why wouldn't I? You told me to." I said as I giggled like a school girl.

"You never called before…I began to think you didn't want to see me or talk to me at all." Gabriel said quietly.

"I guess I was waiting for you to call me. I don't like bugging people, I thought maybe you didn't want to talk to me!" I said as I laughed.

"Well, I guess we rowed the same boat there." Gabriel began to laugh, "And, that isn't the first time we rowed a boat together." He continued.

"Don't remind me!" I said trying to change that subject real quick.

"There is so much we can do while you are here, either in Los Angeles, or in Santa Monica, pretty much whatever you want, but you have to come to my club." He insisted.

"I'd love to; it's been a long time since I have been to a club." I said excitingly.

I know I was excited, I could hear it in my own voice. The concept and reality of it hadn't hit me yet. We talked for an hour about nothing really; I couldn't keep sharing my excitement to be taking a real vacation.

"I have to go to Los Angeles on Friday, so Josh will pick you up from the Los Angeles International Airport. He will take you to the hotel in Santa Monica. I won't be back until later in the evening or I'd come with him to pick you up, I hope that's okay?" He asked.

"That's fine with me, but I have to be back by Sunday of the next week because my girls have a play at church I really want to see. They have been practicing for weeks." I said twisting my hair into a loose curl.

"That's fine; I can make your return flight whenever you need to be home. You can leave as early as Saturday night or very early Sunday morning, just let me know." He said as he whispered something to someone near him.

"Sounds like you are busy, I will let you go." I said but really didn't want to get off the phone.

"Okay, I'm sorry; I was just telling Josh to make sure that he got tickets for the right plane flight." He said as he said something else but I couldn't hear it.

"Once again Gabriel, thank you." I said because I didn't know what else to say.

"I can't wait to see you! I'll call you Friday morning before I leave for my meeting." Gabriel said with warmth in his voice.

It took all the courage I had in the world not to tell him about all the nights I spent with other people wishing I were with him, all the memories I had that never left my mind, and how I truly felt-but, I didn't, I just said goodbye and hung up.

I spent the next few days putting things together, and spending as much time as I could with the girls doing things we normally didn't do just because I wasn't depressed or maybe because I had so much excitement inside me that I didn't know what to do with it.

"Mommy, grandma said you were going on vacation to visit an old friend but papaw said you were chasing a crazy dream, what does chasing a crazy dream mean?" My daughter Rayanne asked me one night while I pushed her in the swing at the park. The curls in her long brown hair were flowing in the wind.

"Papaw is silly Rayanne" I laughed, "When mommy was a bit younger than you, I went to my grandma's house in Florida for a few months out of the summer and I had a very best friend there, his name was Gabriel. I have some pictures of him at grandmas…." I stopped for a second and thought about what I was going to say next…after all, this was my daughter I was talking to, the girl who had no connection to Gabriel but in so many ways, lived her life not knowing how much I loved him.

"Chasing a dream just means that papaw THINKS I am going on vacation to fall in love." I said sweetly.

"People go on vacation to fall in love mommy?" Rayanne asked so innocently.

"Some people do, some people go to get away, and I look at it like the opportunity to have some mommy time." I firmly told her.

"Oh, so papaw was right when he said you were going to find yourself?" She asked.

Under my breathe I said to myself, *I'm going to choke my parents for having conversations about me when I'm not around* .

"Can I meet him some day?" She asked sweetly.

"Maybe one day you will." I said back hoping my dreams to be with him might come true.

Rayanne seemed content with the end of the conversation so I left it at that. I really did want to call my dad and ask him to explain to my eight year old why I longed for something that didn't even exist, but I didn't call him. I found myself extremely nervous as time crept up on me.

On Friday I made sure that I had everything, double checking the windows and doors in the house, making sure the girls had everything they needed. I hated to leave all my dirty laundry but I didn't have time to wash it and put it all away. Gabriel called me at ten in the morning just as he said he would, told me which hotel I would be staying at and that my key card would be at the front with my name on it.

He told me to have a safe flight and he would see me that evening. If he had called me at ten, it must have been seven in the morning his time because I am almost certain that California is three hours behind Tennessee. I hadn't been that nervous since my high school speech class, I got over that doing PR work but I still remember the feeling.

Chapter 4-The Start of Vacation

I took the girls to my parents and told them to behave although deep down I knew it wasn't going to happen. I started to think about how they would act and if they were going to drive my parents insane. I figured it would be more so my mother because my father would just go work in the garage. I patted Cairo on his head and rubbed his belly. I listened to my mom lecture me for about a half hour when my dad grabbed my shoulders, put me in the car, and drove off while my mother was still talking. Cairo was wagging his tail and the girls were waving.

My father was on the phone with his boss the entire ride to the Nashville Airport and I almost felt like he did that on purpose so he didn't have to talk to me about the trip. I wasn't sure there was much I wanted to say to him about it anyway.

Maybe he thought I had heard enough from my mother. My father was a short man, he had a burly beard and wasn't what you would strike him to be upon hearing his voice on the phone.

He never said much to me; but I suppose we both shared universal ideas, I was just afraid to talk about them. As he stopped in front of the airport, he pushed me out of the car and waved as he drove off-still on the phone. I suppose he thought I was going to change my mind. My plane left at 5:00, it was about a four hour flight from Nashville to Los Angeles, which would mean that it would be 9:00 my time, 6:00 their time.

I was trying to decide if I was going to change my watch when I got there or if I should do it now. All I kept thinking about was how I was going to act or respond to all of this. I took a short nap on the plane, but the excitement of it all made me less and less tired. I tried to keep from thinking about how wonderful this vacation was going to be.

When I landed, Josh met me at the gate and directed me to the car. It was the nicest car I had planted my rear in, who drives a Mercedes Benz GL? I mean, I always liked the Cadillac Escalade but it was too pricy for me; I always wanted to own one but I never could afford it. I had a new car, but it definitely didn't cost that much. I was afraid to get in. I stood there staring at it while Josh took my bags. After the initial shock wore off, which was after he shut the trunk, we started the 25-30 minute drive to Santa Monica.

The drive to the hotel was pretty cool, Josh didn't say much but we had the same taste in music, every song was one I knew and loved, I tried to refrain from singing so I just looked out of the window at all the places I had never seen and everything I wanted to do while I was there. I wanted to stay in Los Angeles, not because Gabriel was there, but because I had never been and I had only seen Los Angeles through movies or magazines.

"Thank you so much for picking me up and bringing me to the hotel, I appreciate it" I said as I jumped out of the car.

"Your welcome; and I believe Gabriel left you a note with your key card at the front desk so make sure you get it." Josh said with a light smile as he got out and took my things out of the trunk.

Josh wasn't as cute as Gabriel and Spencer, but he seemed nice; he was short. Well, probably 5'9, that's taller than me, but I always had a thing for boys who were taller than me, I even liked football because most of the quarterbacks were over 6'3, and the younger ones were so hot.

As he drove off, I realized that I had only put two bags in the very back and had kept three with me in the backseat. SHIT! I was so excited that I left half my stuff in the back seat of Josh's car! Luckily I still had my purse or it would have been a disaster not having an ID to prove I was who I said I was and what *if* I had forgotten my purse? I had to get it together! I would have been stuck, I didn't have Gabriel's phone number memorized, *if* I had left my purse, I would have really been screwed. I didn't even have Spencer's card, it was on my desk at work.

I went to the front desk of this very nice hotel and gave them my ID. They gave me my card and a note from Gabriel. Funny, his hand writing hadn't changed much. He still doted his I's the same, and signed his name the same, "Always, Gabriel." It just said that he would be back in town around 8:00 and Josh would pick me back up around 9:00 to take me to the club he owns. I went to my room to take a short nap before I had to get ready. I started figuring out the time difference, it was 6:40 now; I could take a nap, then get up at 8:00 and make myself look good.

When I woke up I realized I had slept longer than I wanted to, it was 8:30! I jumped in the shower and hurried to get ready. 9:00 came and went. My heart was racing. *Why can't there be more hours in a day?* It was 12:00 a.m. my time and I was still really tired. Josh knocked on my hotel room door about 9:30 and I still felt like I wasn't ready. We headed down stairs and got into the car.

"You know you left your stuff in the backseat?" Josh laughed.

"I realized that after I left! I was so excited to be here that I forgot to grab it, I'm so sorry!" I told Josh as I looked him directly in the eye with the most sincerity. He had blue eyes too, but not near as beautiful or deep blue as Gabriel's.

"It's cool, Gabriel won't care." Josh replied.

"This is Gabriel's car?" I exclaimed.

"Yeah, I take every opportunity to drive his cars." Josh laughed as we headed to the club.

He has more than one, what did I get myself into? I thought.

We got to the club around 10:00 and Josh let me out in front of the building. It did look pretty small. I met a security guard at the door. He told me I couldn't get in without a card. Josh just dropped me off and I had no idea what I was supposed to say or do. So there I was, standing on a busy street with a thigh high skirt on, a white see thru shirt, white stilettos, and then had to thumb through my purse looking for my phone to call Gabriel.

Just as I began to search my purse, Josh walked up and told the security guard to let me in. Josh handed me a card that looked similar to a credit card, but heavier.

We both walked in together, I walked past the front door and it opened up into a huge club. *Small club? What was Gabriel's definition of a big club?* The place was insanely busy. There were people at both bars lined up waiting for drinks.

I walked past the dance floor to the bathroom to make sure I looked okay. I guess I expected Gabriel to meet me there and it kind of made me uncomfortable. After I left the bathroom, I made my way back to the entry hallway. There were mirrors everywhere but they were playing some awesome music, the most current hip hop. I loved it.

I wished Nora was there because I could have danced my way around all of these people. I looked to my left and the bar in the corner had two bartenders and people all around it. I thought to myself, *should I get a drink?*

Everyone was dressed very nice, but they looked like a mix of elite people, some were in business suits sitting off side talking, holding cocktails, it looked like they were conducting business. Some people looked like normal everyday people I might see in Tennessee. Right by the front door was another bar I must have missed when I came in, I noticed the restroom sign and walked right past it. I had to look twice because it appeared that Spencer was bartending by himself. *Was he a bartender?* I thought.

There was a line about ten people long waiting on drinks, he looked frustrated, I didn't see Gabriel anywhere, and the people standing in line looked mad. I walked over to Spencer and stopped at the open end of the bar.

"Spencer, where is Gabriel?" I yelled above the music.

"In a meeting upstairs," He said as he looked up at me, then down again and pointed up.

I looked up and there was a cat walk that circled the entire club and I could see a glass wall behind it.

"You guys look busy, is it like this all the time?" I yelled out to him.

"Two bartenders called off tonight, and here I am." Spencer yelled back sharply.

He seemed like he might not want to be bothered by my questions at that point in time and I could understand that. I kind of took it personal, but not to the heart. I realized he was busy. His fore head was nothing but beads of sweat, and I really thought the air could have circulated better. I wasn't getting that same beautiful smile he gave me in Tennessee, maybe he would be nicer if Gabriel was around, maybe he was stressed.

"Do you need some help?" I asked him, yelling again.

"Do you know anything about bartending?" Spencer looked directly at my chest and said.

"Not really but I can pour beer pretty well." I said redirecting his eyes to mine. I kicked off my stilettos and walked behind the bar.

"What happens if you drop something on your foot?" He said as he looked down at my bare feet.

"I guess it will hurt." I said with a smile.

He smiled back and continued to finish the drink he was making. We stood in the same spot for about two hours, I never seen Gabriel once during that time and I really thought it was rude, *I thought he said he would be back at eight?* I kept looking at my watch, in which I set for California time, it was now midnight.

Thinking about Gabriel was put on hold for a short period of time because I really wanted to help Spencer so I continued to bust my ass pouring liquor and beer. Spencer and I didn't really say too much to each other until I opened a bottle of wine with some really odd looking cork screw and the cork popped out at Spencer, hitting him in the face. He stopped making a drink, turned to me with a blank look on his face and then busted out in laughter.

"That's the most excitement I've had all night." We both laughed and from that point on we made a game out of it.

I forgot Gabriel was missing in action; after all, Spencer was superhot. He had dark hair, hazel eyes, he looked like he worked out, I would say he weighed about 240 and had a smile that would make you melt. I really didn't mind being in a confined space with him. He had on jeans, a tee shirt, and white tennis shoes. He sparked my curiosity but I tried not to get too close to him, he had to have a girlfriend somewhere nearby.

"So-you bartend?" I asked him inquisitively.

"Not really, I have just had enough drinks in my life to know what goes in them." He laughed.

The music suddenly began to slow down. The hip hop had gone off and slow pop music came on. This was my kind of place; I began to think I was in the wrong occupation. I loved music; I should have been working at a club.

People would order a drink and tell me to keep the change. More money ran through my hands than I made in a week. People were slow dancing on the dance floor and things at the bar got calmer. It wasn't as loud as it had been so I started talking to him.

"How was your trip to Florida?" I asked.

"I was pissed because I wanted to stop and see my family but we didn't have time. Gabriel has a huge project going on and it's been pretty time consuming." He said.

"Your parents live in Florida?" I asked.

"Yes, in Sarasota." He responded.

Sarasota? How did I miss that one?

"How long did you live in Sarasota?" I asked.

"My whole life." He responded as he started cleaning off the bar counter.

"I miss Sarasota. It was so beautiful." I said as I grabbed a towel and started at the other end.

"You would love the pier then, it's beautiful. It reminds me of Florida." He smiled.

The music began to pick up again, as did the line. A really great song came on and I started dancing while pouring beer. Spencer started laughing at me.

"You're not the one wearing beer here so shut it." I said to him laughing.

"Oh yeah, I forgot, this huge bruise I have from that cork on my face doesn't count for something does it?" Spencer laughed again.

"You can't even see it but it counts for me not being able to open a bottle of wine with your jacked up wine opener ever again." I said sarcastically as I looked at his face for the alleged bruise.

Spencer must have been feeling the next song that came on because he walked behind me, grabbed my waist as he reached for a bottle of liquor, then danced behind me for a few seconds. The guys getting drinks started cheering him on, I just went with it and laughed. I was having fun doing something I knew nothing about. *Wait! What if he does have a girlfriend floating around here? Well, he was playing with me first.* I thought.

"I want to dance so bad I can't stand it." I said.

"So, go dance." Spencer pointed to the dance floor.

"I am not going out there to dance by myself." I continued. "Dance with me." I smiled.

"I don't dance." Spencer said sharply.

"Awe, you weren't just dancing with me?" I laughed as I continued making drinks.

"That wasn't dancing." Spencer said as he moved to the other end of the bar.

"Did I touch a nerve?" I yelled as I smiled.

"Nope, just don't dance." Spencer said again. "But I do poke people when they keep asking me the same question." Spencer moved closer to me and started poking me in the side. I tried to cover my sides but that didn't work. He just followed me around everywhere I moved, poking me. He was obviously a lot stronger than me so grabbing his wrist to get him to stop was a complete failure.

"Stop it!" I yelled laughing.

"Why?" He said smiling.

"Because I said so…" I stopped moving around as he continued to poke me.

"I don't want to." He said as he poked me some more.

"I'm going to pee myself." I laughed as I hunched over in a ball.

"Why?" He asked as he stopped.

"Why what?" I said as I punched him in the arm.

Gabriel finally made his appearance and I saw him out of the corner of my eye just as Spencer started chasing me around the bar with an open bottle of champagne. I felt sick to my stomach just seeing him. I was a mess. I was sweaty, my clothes were soaked and my feet hurt so badly. If we had been having a wet tee shirt contest, I would have won. My see thru shirt was really seeing through-to my bra.

"What are you doing?" Gabriel said laughing.

"Whattt's it look like I'm doing?" I said back laughing.

"Casey and Nevara never showed up?" Gabriel said as he leaned over the bar top to yell to Spencer.

"I haven't seen either of them, if it weren't for Kensie, I would have gone nuts." Spencer said back to Gabriel as he put the champagne bottle down and started washing glasses.

"I'm sending Seth and Alex over to finish up the evening and you can go back to doing what you do best. Thanks for helping out Kensie, join me?" Gabriel said as he held out his hand to mine to help me from behind the bar.

"Here." Gabriel said as he handed me a shirt that had the clubs name on it.

"What's that for?" I inquired with a confused look on my face.

"You can see straight through your shirt, worse because it's wet." He laughed.

"Oh, yeah" I said as I looked at my chest. "Thanks."

I put the shirt on over my shirt, I had a tank on under the see thru one, but it was silk and it was sticking to me. My feet hurt so bad that I didn't even want to put my shoes back on. I walked barefoot across the dance floor as Gabriel led me hand in hand to the VIP room on the other side. People were staring at us, I thought maybe they were looking at me in my bare feet which made me self-conscious, but I soon realized it wasn't my feet they were looking at. Gabriel and I sat down and he ordered a couple of drinks from the waitress. I laughed.

"What's so funny?" Gabriel asked seriously.

"The fact that you just ordered drinks from the waitress is funny to me, I'm sorry." I said back with a witty smile.

"Thanks for helping out tonight. I am really sorry I didn't get down here; there was an issue with a screen play we have been working on. How was your flight?" Gabriel asked changing the subject.

"It was okay, getting in the club was the worst part. If it hadn't been for Josh, I'd probably be sitting curb side and about that…" I said and stopped.

"About what?" He said with a curious look on his face.

"You work for a production company? You are the production company AND you own a huge club, you said it was little. I guess you neglected to tell me exactly how important you are." I said sarcastically.

"It does look little, from the outside. It was nice to talk to someone I knew from long ago that didn't judge me or put me on a pedestal because I produce movies. It was so nice just to talk to you like we did long ago without that interference." Gabriel said.

"I understand that, I guess it's just a bit over whelming but I am so proud of you! It looks like you have made all of your dreams come true!" I exclaimed as I leaned forward and grabbed his wrist.

"I only wonder where we might be if your grandma had not passed away when she did. I think we would have always kept in touch; but I'm glad you are here now and that you found me. I can't say that it didn't occur to me to find you-I just don't have a lot of time to do anything anymore. After you left that day in Florida, I knew deep in my heart I would never see you again. I tried not to ponder on it, but part of me died that day and I never really stopped thinking about what a great friend you were to me." Gabriel said seriously.

He seemed really heart felt, almost teary eyed.

"I will give you the shirt back when it absorbs all this sweat. Gross." I said pulling at the shirt and changing the subject because I didn't really know what to say.

"I'm surprised Spencer didn't give you one before now, but I'm sure it made your tips better." He laughed.

"Maybe, people were throwing money around loosely." I laughed back.

"I am glad you found me when you did because awhile back, I honestly probably wouldn't have seen it. That was the first time in a while that I checked that web site. Usually I'm on my email every day; wish you would have had that long ago. I was pretty excited when I saw that friend request, I must admit." Gabriel changed the subject again.

"I was glad I found you as well. It was really weird to talk to you the first time." I said.

"I think your agency can help me with my new movie and I really am thinking of hiring them to be a promoter. We need a country song in one scene so maybe you guys can help, and getting some extra's in the film." Gabriel shifted the conversation to business.

"That would be really cool. We could use the business, and if you are serious, I have to get you in to talk to the owner because he finalizes everything." I added.

"That would be good, you look really great by the way, and I really can't believe how much you have grown. From a frizzy brown haired girl full of laughter, you grew up quite well." Gabriel said with a smile.

"I would love to say this is how I looked when I came in, but it isn't. I have managed to spill beer all over me." I said as I looked down at my lap.

"I know, I seen you when you came in, I just couldn't get away from that meeting, you looked great. Are you hungry? Do you want to get something to eat?" Gabriel asked.

"I'd love to, I am really hungry." I smiled while sipping my drink. I didn't even know what it was, it tasted like it had vodka in it; maybe it was a martini.

Finally, I get to hang out with him, I thought, *hopefully it won't be business related.*

"I'm going to take Spencer with us since he busted his ass all night at the bar, if that's okay with you?" Gabriel asked as he grabbed my hand and held it.

"Sure, he was a lot of fun in a strange situation!" I said.

Gabriel yelled to Josh but he didn't hear him. I suppose he was going to tell him to get Spencer for him since he was standing 5 feet from us. Spencer had decided to sit at the bar and drink a beer. He had taken off the first shirt and now had on a new tank top. Yankees.

Both of them? I thought. His muscles were huge. He had several tattoos on his upper arms but I couldn't make them out. They weren't tacky; they looked like tribal art, same as Gabriel's.

There were girls flocked to him like glue, which was to be expected, I mean, he's sitting at the bar in a tank top and a pair of jeans soaked from sweat. He was a hot mess but the whores loved it, okay, maybe they weren't whores, but they were basically sitting in his lap. He was smiling, carrying on conversations with them; one of the girls leaned in and whispered something in his ear. He laughed and went back to his drink. Gabriel finally got tired of yelling for Josh and pulled his phone out from his pocket.

"Since Josh can't hear me to grab Spencer, I'm calling him." Gabriel laughed.

"I can't believe you are calling him from across the room. You are lazy." I said laughing.

"I know; it was easier than leaving you alone, again, even for a second." Gabriel laughed.

His drink sat still, not even being touched. I wondered why he ordered it; but then I thought, it didn't matter, it was his club anyway.

I watched Spencer pull his phone out from his pocket and turn to look around to see where Gabriel was. They both laughed. Spencer got up from the bar and walked towards us. At least four girls stopped him before he got there, he smiled and kept walking. Gabriel got his keys from Josh and the three of us left the club through the back door. He opened the car door for me and then shut it. We went to a pub not far from his club.

"I want to pay you for working for me tonight." Gabriel said when we sat down.

"I don't want your money Gabriel. I was just helping out." I said sharply.

"She did a great job for not knowing what she was doing." Spencer said with a smile.

I had taken my shoes off under the table because my feet were killing me. I had Spencer on one side of me, his knee was touching my leg, but I'm not sure if he noticed it or not. Gabriel was on the other side, holding my hand under the table. We ordered drinks and appetizers. We talked for over an hour about our fishing trips, and Gabriel had to bring up the fact that I fell in the channel once trying to catch a fish.

"I actually have pictures of that, I really do; I was soaked!" I said with embarrassment. "That was my first camera, and I just had to have it THAT day." I smiled.

"It was the greatest thing I have ever seen!" Gabriel turned in to Spencer to say.

"I bet...about like the time she snagged her own ass with a hook?" Spencer chimed in.

"You told him about that?" I said with complete animosity.

"Oh yeah! I tell everyone I know that story." Gabriel started laughing so hard he almost choked.

"Wish I'd been there." Spencer said as he bought another round of drinks and pushed his leg closer to mine. He had to have known he was touching me, if I felt it; he had to have felt it too.

I was starving but the nachos we ate and mozzarella sticks weren't too appealing. I figured I would just eat a huge breakfast at the hotel in the morning. I filled up on Margarita's for the time being. I have to admit, I don't drink that often, definitely couldn't stand on my own against those two. They each had four beers so far; I had two margaritas and was feeling pretty good by now. It was getting pretty late, or early, it was 3:00 the last time I checked my watch.

"The only thing I never got to do in Florida was swim with the dolphins. My parents would never let me do that, or get on Jet Ski's." I said breaking the silence.

"That is the most exciting thing ever!" Spencer exclaimed with a heartfelt smile.

His hair was so messy in the front that I just wanted to fix it for him, but I didn't say anything. At that point, Gabriel had his hand on my chair, my palms were so sweaty, and I began to wonder what I was going to do if he tried to kiss me when I went back to the hotel. His phone rang and he excused himself from the table. I just kept staring at him, he was so hot. Spencer and I continued the conversation without Gabriel but I didn't take my eyes off him.

"You have swum with the dolphins?" I asked still staring at Gabriel in the corner on his phone.

"Yeah, in Florida; you can't really do it in Santa Monica unless you make an appointment to do it privately. The fish people don't really like people interacting with dolphins. In the wild, they will poke you with their nose if they are in the water with you, sometimes." Spencer said as he turned in towards me and took a bite of nacho.

"The FISH people?" I said laughing as I looked at Spencer.

"Yeah, the fish people. I always wanted to ride a horse, but never did." Spencer said.

"You have never ridden a horse?" I said surprised.

"Nope." Spencer said sharply.

"You should come to Tennessee, riding a horse is so amazing and you can just about do that anywhere." I said.

"That would be cool, if I'm ever that way again." Spencer changed the subject. "So, the next time you come to the club, I am going to introduce you to some of the girls who work there so you can dance. I know you wanted to, and there are a couple of girls there who are really cool." Spencer added.

Gabriel returned to the table. He said he had to excuse himself because he had an issue at the club he had to take care of. He leaned down and said something to Spencer and then turned to me, kissed me on the forehead and said he would call a cab to take me to the hotel.

"We will take a cab back to the club after we finish these drinks and I will take her to the hotel, if that's okay with you, Kensie?" Spencer asked.

"If you don't mind, I think my things are still in Gabriel's back seat." I promptly told him.

"We will get it out at the club and I will take you to the hotel." Spencer repeated.

"I'm very sorry I have to take off, I will make it up to you." Gabriel leaned down, kissed my forehead again and left.

Every time he did that I wanted to cry. I just wanted to lie next to him, listen to his heart beat, and fall asleep in a comfort zone.

"He doesn't stay in once place for too long, does he?" I asked Spencer.

"Not really, he moves around a lot. I think he has adult ADHD." Spencer noted.

"I'd be so irritated if I led his life." I said frowning.

"I'm sure this has been a horrible trip for you already, and I'm sorry for that." Spencer said

"It's only day one, I have plenty of time…there are so many things I want to do and see while I am here, even if Gabriel is busy. While driving to the hotel, I observed several places I want to go. It's okay, really." I said with complete sincerity.

After we finished our drinks, we sat for a while in silence. Foreigners "I want to know what love is" was playing in the background as it started to grow quiet. It was a bit uncomfortable for me and I wasn't sure why. It wasn't like Spencer and I came here together, without Gabriel. I guess I was a bit backwards, pretty outgoing, unless I thought the guy was superhot; then I stumbled over my words. Spencer started looking around the room as people began to leave.

I looked around at all the couples that were slow dancing, or leaving together. Some came together; some just met. I thought I should have been one of those people, leaving with someone too, if only for a night, if only for...forever. I wanted to sing the song, but I couldn't. I started sort of humming it to myself...

"In my life, there's been heart ache and pain, I don't know if I can face it again, can't stop now, I've traveled so far, to change this lonely life...I want to know what love is, I want you to show me..." I looked up at Spencer and he was now staring at me.

I was glad Gabriel had left because if I had heard that song play, and he had been there, it might have upset me. I would have probably given the lyrics too much thought and he probably wouldn't have even paid any attention to it. I began to feel myself getting on an unpredictable theme park ride of emotions...where would it lead me? I wanted to cry but wanted to laugh. I would look up at Spencer, then around at the bar, he would look at me, I could sense it, then do the same thing I was doing.

"I suppose I should ask you if you want to dance although it's against my better judgement." Spence said calmly.

"I don't slow dance, but thanks for asking." I said back with half a smile because I felt like he only asked because he thought it was appropriate.

"That's good, I didn't want to anyway." He said and smiled.

"I know you didn't." I said back as we both laughed.

Things were quiet again and a lot of silence was between us. So much silence you could have cut it open.

"What?" I asked Spencer smiling when our eyes met.

"Nothing." Spencer said as he smiled back.

"Do I have something on my face?" I asked as I started sweeping my mouth with my hand.

"No, you don't." Spencer said as he took his hand up to my eye and swept my hair from my face. That felt weird to me, I always thought boys who swept a girls hair from her face must really like them. I had no idea why he was staring at me, it made me nervous.

Spencer reached into his pocket as he cleared his throat and handed me some money. I looked at him strangely.

"What is that for?" I asked Spencer.

"Gabriel wanted me to give you some money for helping out tonight." Spencer said.

"I am not taking that. I don't want it. It was a fun experience for me, I should pay him." I said as I laughed, "All I really want is some real food tomorrow. I am starving!" I finished.

"I guess Gabriel didn't think about you being on a plane and not eating most of the evening, and working so hard, it made me hungry as hell." He said with that big, beautiful smile. "I would have taken you to get some real food, but that's just me." He finished.

"Uh, yeah, I think that was the hardest I've physically worked in years." I laughed.

"Are you about ready to head back?" Spencer asked as he stood up and the chair scratched across the floor.

"Sure, I am really tired." I said as I stood up as well.

I grabbed my purse off the table and checked the time. By now it was 4:30 in the morning. I couldn't remember the last time I had been awake at that hour. It was 7:30 back home; I had two short naps in twenty four hours! He walked over to the waitress and was talking to her. Odd I thought. He was giving her his beautiful smile. Everything seemed to be moving in slow motion. Maybe I was just really buzzing.

"He paid the tab, I guess." Spencer said shrugging his shoulders as he walked back towards me.

"That was nice of him; I would have paid for mine." I said back shrugging mine.

"Gabriel wouldn't have let you anyway; he really has no concept of money." Spencer said as he put his hand on my back and led me outside.

"Must be nice." I said as we walked out the door.

Spencer grabbed a cab when we went outside and we rode back to the club. He sat on one side looking out the window; I sat one the other side looking straight ahead. I observed everything. When we got to the club Spencer got out and came over to open my door...I had no idea he was going to do that so I was half way out before he got around the cab. We walked over to Gabriel's car; Spencer unlocked it and opened the door. I got my bags out of the back seat and Spencer took them from me. Who were these people? I felt like I had been living on an isolated island for years with indigenous people and just found civilization. I am sure I looked at Spencer with a dazed look...he just smiled and shook his head. At this point I had no idea what happened to me...I became silent, I felt like I couldn't feel my body, like I was an orb floating through space. I couldn't explain it to him, all I could do is move in slow motion. Spencer started walking and I slowly followed him.

"Are you going to walk behind me or with me?" Spencer said as he laughed and turned around. He stopped about 10 feet from Gabriel's car and opened the passenger door of his car. What is it with these boys and their cars? Spencer was driving a silver Lotus Elise.

Wow. They must make some decent money. I would never own a car like this. I really felt insecure like I had no business being there. I work with the rich, I'm not the rich. I guess when you have money at hand, you get what you want.

You still can't buy love; it might make some people happy for the moment, but do they really love? A friend of mine in high school loved money, she never loved herself or

anyone else. I don't judge them, I guess I'm a bit jealous,
I've struggled for a while, but I know some day everything
will be better.

Spencer drove me to the hotel and didn't say much on the
way there. He made acute conversation about Santa Monica
but nothing major. When we got to the hotel, he jumped out
and ran around the car to open my door.

"Ha Ha! I got it that time!" He said as he let out this loud
goofy almost fake laugh.

"Nice…it won't happen next time." I said as I laughed.
He just shook his head and gave me that big beautiful smile.
We walked beside each other into the hotel and he carried
my three goofy bags I forgot to the elevator. He seemed
really sweet. I saw him making a waving motion with his
hand out of the corner of my eye.

I looked over and he was pointing to the lady on the
elevator standing beside me. I stepped back next to him and
looked at her. She had her skirt tucked into her panties. I
almost pissed myself. I had to cover my mouth to keep from
laughing out loud.

His smile was dreamy; he had the cutest dimple on the left
side. His smile was starting to grow on me. After I got to
my room, Spencer said good night, handed me my bags and
left. I kind of thought Gabriel would have been the one to
walk me to my hotel room, but Spencer did the situation
justice too. My vacation wasn't off to a great start, but not a
bad one either.

Chapter 5-Spencer

As soon as I walked into the room, I face planted the bed. I think I fell asleep in mid-air. I woke up at 10:30 and called my parents to check on the girls. They didn't miss me. They didn't even talk to me for longer than ten minutes.

I asked how Cairo was doing; I missed him lying next to me. Dad said he was doing fine in the garage and he even let him come in the house last night. Everything seemed to be in order; I knew I needed to stop worrying about them.

After I got off the phone with my dad, I put on some short denim shorts and a tank top. I forgot my tennis shoes so my flip flops had to do. I pulled my hair back into a pony tail and decided to walk down the strip since Gabriel had not called, I hoped everything was okay. I hadn't heard from him since he left the pub. I was like a child in the biggest toy store in New York; it was like a painting in Italy, I marveled at everything I didn't see every day…the people, the shops, the beauty. I stopped at a café to get a coffee, there were two lines; they both were long.

I stood there for fifteen minutes when I turned to my left and why in the world was Spencer standing right next to me in line? I didn't even notice it.

"That's funny, I just went to the hotel to take you out to breakfast and you definitely did not answer the door." Spencer said without turning his head at all.

"Are you stalking me?" I laughed.

"Nope, just came here for coffee and I was about to call Gabriel and get your number so I could see what you were doing. "I didn't expect you to go prancing around places you have never been." Spencer said with seriousness.

"I'm a big girl, I can handle my own." I said with sarcasm.

"I see." He said as he stood there with his arms crossed in front of him but never turned to look towards me.

We both grabbed our coffees and walked out of the café to the seats outside. The street was busy and the sun was shining. It was a gorgeous day.

"What are your plans for the day? Gabriel is still asleep so don't plan to hear from him anytime soon. He was at the club until seven this morning." Spencer stated as he pulled out a chair for me to sit.

"Why was he there so late, is everything okay?" I asked sitting down. I wasn't used to boys opening doors and pulling chairs in and out for me.

"Money came up missing in the bar drawer and it took them like two hours to track it down." Spencer said.

"The drawer WE were using?" I asked in astonishment.

"Yes, but they found it. It was in the drop under the drawer, did you drop it there?" Spencer said with a smile.

"I did, the drawer got full and I put a bunch of hundreds throughout the night in the slot under the drawer." I said with a blank look on my face because I felt horrible.

"It's okay, we normally don't drop money; Gabriel usually has one of the bartenders take it to the office." Spencer said with reprimand. "He isn't mad or anything, it's okay, no worries!" He smiled.

"Geez, I hope he didn't think I took it; that would have been awful!" I was embarrassed at this point.

"He didn't. Its fine" He said as he grabbed my arm to reassure me. "He called me and asked why the drawer was a grand short when I got home and I told him I had no idea. I understand you not wanting to take the money Gabriel wanted me to give you but will you at least take half of what we made?" Spencer touched the side of my face and pushed my head up gently looking me directly in the eyes.

"I really don't want it. I swear to you, I really don't." I said again putting my head back down.

"That's cool because I didn't keep your part and I thought you would say that so I got you something. It's in my car; I'll give it to you later." Spencer smiled.

"What is it?" I asked with excitement. I wasn't used to people giving me gifts. I wasn't into materialistic things and I didn't expect anything from anyone. I wasn't used to any of this trip and I found myself in deep thought.

"You'll find out later and you never answered me about your plans for the day." Spencer quickly changed the subject as he stood up to throw his empty coffee cup in the trash.

"Kensie?" He said as he stood beside me.

"I'm sorry, what did you say?" I asked returning to reality and looking up at him.

"What are your plans for the day?" He asked again.

"Well, I passed this art museum earlier, after that, nothing." I said as stood up to throw away my coffee cup but it wasn't empty.

"Mind if I join you?" Spencer asked.

"Not at all, I'd love it." I exclaimed.

"I know you have to be hungry, we could go back in the café and order some lunch," he said as he pointed behind him, "and then go to the art museum; I know which one you're talking about." Spencer said as he stood closely next to me.

"You know, I really am not that hungry right now, but I'm not sure why." I said with a rumbling in my stomach but I really didn't think I could eat anything, I felt odd to be hanging out with him to begin with, I liked him, but I was there to spend time with Gabriel and I normally didn't connect with guys like I did Spencer.

"Okay, well, let's go to the art museum and then we can go to the Santa Monica pier and have lunch there." Spencer said as he started to walk back up the strip.

"Okay, sounds good to me." I caught up to him and we walked side by side. People were looking at us, at least I felt like they were. I felt guilty but I wasn't really with Gabriel, it's not like I was dating anyone, but for some reason I kept looking at my phone.

"Waiting for a phone call from your boyfriend?" Spencer said as he laughed. I don't think he really wanted an answer.

"No, I don't have a boyfriend." I laughed, "That's the funniest thing I have ever heard." I finished.

"Why is that funny? You're a beautiful girl; I'm surprised you aren't married." Spencer blurted out.

"Been there and done that...no thanks." I said sarcastically.

"Did I touch a nerve?" He said as he laughed and pushed me with his index finger.

"Uh, no..." I laughed back knowing he was saying that because of what I said about him dancing.

"You seem kind of hard on yourself." He said.

"Why do I seem hard on myself?" I asked.

"I see it on your face, paranoia." He said as he grabbed my arm and pulled me to the left side of the street to cross.

"I don't have time for that, between work and the girls, AND school, I really don't do much. I haven't really been out in a while." I said with hostility.

"Everyone has time for attention; you must just not want it." He said with a huge smile.

"Wanting it and making time for it are two different things..." I snarled.

"I see." Spencer said as he bumped me while we were walking. We didn't say anything else to each other the entire walk to the Santa Monica Museum of Art.

When we got there, Spencer opened the door for me and the place was absolutely beautiful.

"My father painted when I was younger but I haven't seen him paint in years." I said to him to break the silence. The paintings at the museum were phenomenal.

"You know, I have never been in here." He said.

"It's just, I can't explain it. Art is so incredibly interesting. It's like you have to wonder what they were thinking when they created their work. It's almost like music, beautifully written by someone who carried a thought to paper." I added.

"I was never much into art, but I love music so I can understand your line of thinking." Spencer said. "If you find the right person, they can be fascinating too." Spencer said as he looked at me.

After a while, I could tell he was getting bored so I suggested lunch. He agreed and called a cab to the Santa Monica Pier.

Spencer looked incredibly hot, and the cab ride to the beach was exciting too, Spencer pointed out some interesting sites along the way and we laughed at some of the people on the street.

We ended up going to 'Back on the Beach Café.' It was strange because I felt like I knew Spencer, but at the same time, I was feeling a little skeptical for being there with him because I didn't really know him. I felt, comfortable and weird at the same time. I was back on that emotional roller coaster.

"What do you think of Santa Monica?" He asked while we sat down at our table.

"Well, it's a lot different than Tennessee; there are a lot of places to shop. Could have sworn I seen an actual actor but I'm not sure if it was him. I didn't ask." I said as I laughed.

"It's possible, we aren't far from LA." Spencer said with a smile.

"What are you going to have for lunch?" I asked Spencer hoping he would suggest something.

"I'm not sure, something light since we are going to the pier." He said as he looked over the menu.

The waiter came over and asked if we were ready and I ordered a chicken salad. Spencer said he wanted the same thing. We really didn't say much while we were waiting for lunch, just some minor conversation about the weather and Santa Monica.

"So, are you a sports girl?" Spencer asked when our food came.

"Love sports. I love football, and baseball, of course." I smiled.

"Gabriel and I have always liked the Yankees. I guess I prefer college football, USC or Notre Dame." He said as he continued to eat.

"I always thought of Gabriel whenever I seen someone with anything Yankee's on, he always wore Yankees, glad to see he finally got a new hat." I laughed.

"Some things you never out grow." He said as he stared at me then smiled.

"I always loved the White Sox, and the Braves. I don't watch a lot of basketball, but I sure watched enough boys play it." I said as I took a bite of my salad. I kept wiping my mouth with my napkin to make sure nothing was on my face. I wanted to check my teeth and I prayed to God he didn't have anything on his face or I would have noticed it.

"You like Gabriel don't you?" Spencer smiled.

"I guess that I…" I scampered with my words…"I am excited to be here. I thought of him a lot during my teenage years, he was a big part of my life." I finished.

"I see it in your eyes every time you say his name." Spencer smiled.

"You see a lot in my facial expressions, don't you?" I included.

"I just read people, well; usually I'm right on target." Spencer added.

"I used to think I knew people, but I am finding out as I've gotten older that I really don't. Sometimes you think you know people, and you really don't. I analyze too much, about everything, because I'm used to it." I said.

Spencer got quiet and we finished eating in silence. He would look up at me occasionally with this look in his eyes like he felt sorry for me and I hated it. It could have been my imagination, maybe I *was* paranoid. Maybe he thought I was analyzing him.

"What about you?" I finally asked.

"I have no story…" Spencer said shortly.

"Everyone has some kind of story, it can't be that simple. It's never that simple." I said as I pushed my plate away.

Spencer pushed his finished plate towards the center of the table.

"What's your favorite movie?" He asked changing the subject.

"I don't have one." I said knowing I did but I wasn't going to tell him what it was.

"So what is it then?" He asked again leaning in on the table with his elbows. "A love movie?" He said laughing.

"No one's life ends that perfectly. A love movie is a fantasy that just doesn't exist." I said as I leaned in with my elbow on the table and my hand pressed against my jaw.

"Let's go swimming." He said cutting my sentence off.

"I don't have a suit." I said quickly.

"So, buy one." He said with an attitude. I didn't think I was getting out of it even if I said no. Spencer paid the check and we went next door to get me a suit.

He gave me his perfect smile as we went into the store. I hoped he didn't think I was trying on suits and modeling for him to see the stretch marks on my stomach. I might weigh 135 but my body reeks of babies. I have stretch marks all over my stomach and thighs. I have tried to get rid of them but they are there for good. I have been self-conscious about my body for many years, even pre-baby.

I found a cheap bathing suit, a one piece, the back was cut out, pretty low, all the way down to the bottom with one strap in the middle, and the sides had little slits in them. I grabbed black because everyone knows black makes you look thinner.

I walked out of the fitting room and Spencer was sitting in a chair by the window. He stood up as soon as I headed toward him, reaching in his pocket for his wallet. I grabbed some towels along the way and hurried over to the cashier before he got there. I was not about to let him pay for my suit. I was as pale as a ghost, especially standing next to any one there because they were so dark.

Just as we walked out of the store my cell phone began to ring. I could hear it faintly at the bottom of my purse. After digging it out, it was Gabriel.

"Hello!" I said with excitement.

"Hey sweetie, whatcha doin?" Gabriel said back.

"I'm at the Santa Monica pier with Spencer. We ran into each other at the coffee shop." I said quickly.

"Awesome! It's pretty isn't it?" Gabriel asked.

"It's beautiful. I love it! I keep looking at the amusement park thinking I know that scene from somewhere…wait, isn't that where they filmed 'Lost Boys'?" I questioned.

"I don't know," Gabriel laughed, "It's been awhile since I've seen that movie, but that's funny. Gabriel said.

By this time, Spencer and I began to walk towards to beach. He was in front of me about six feet. I was waiting for him to stop someplace but he kept walking.

"I just got up and started making some phone calls, I have to meet my director, and I wanted to call you and tell you I'd love to take you to dinner tonight about eight?" Gabriel said but asked. It sounded like he was eating toast. He was definitely crunching up something.

"That sounds great!" I said with excitement. "By the way, sorry about dropping that money in the drawer last night, I didn't know." I said softly.

"It's fine; we found it, no big deal…it was just really weird nothing was adding up." He laughed.

"Still, I felt really bad." I said back and stopped.

"I'll let you make it up to me IF you let me talk to Spencer, IF you don't mind he uses your phone so I don't have to call him?" Gabriel laughed.

"Sure, Spencer!" I yelled ahead, he was about ten feet in front of me now.

"Do you want to park it here?" Spencer yelled back.

"Sure, here, it's Gabriel; he wants to talk to you." I said as I jogged closer and handed him my phone.

"Where's your suit?" Spencer asked.

I just threw up my hands and walked to find a bathroom. I stood in front of the mirror for ten minutes trying to decide if I was going to wear the suit or not. I finally got tired of looking at myself and how pale I really was against the black and wrapped a towel around my waist and grabbed my clothes. I got a bit lost on the way back but I spotted Spencer messing with some sand on the beach. He was incredibly hard to miss.

"So, do you know if that is where they shot 'Lost Boys' the movie? It looks familiar." I asked him.

"The Pacific Park? I don't think so, I think it was the Santa Cruz Beach Boardwalk…it's really cool at night. Your suit looks good, oh; I laid your phone next to my clothes over there." He said as he stared at me for a few minutes (or at least I thought he was) and then continued to mess with the sand. He had on sunglasses and looked so hot in the sun.

I threw my towel down and sat down on it. I took my hair tie out and wrapped it around my wrist.

"SO, I guess Gabriel and I are having dinner tonight. I'm pretty excited." I said as I took my flops off.

"That's what he said; hopefully you guys will have some quite time to spend together with no interruptions. He's been crazy busy with that screen play. There were some shooting issues and he's been trying to iron them out. You guys should go see some performing arts on the strip, it's really awesome." Spencer said as he looked towards my way again.

"I still can't get over the fact that he produces movies! I am so amazed at what he has done with his life!" I continued, "The tide is so peaceful to watch, moving in and out." I said and paused for a few minutes while rubbing my chin on my shoulder. "You know, some of the people on this beach look like they lead perfect lives, perfect bodies, perfect hair, and perfect skin." I said as Spencer began looking around.

"Perfection is as close as the heart allows it to be." He said freely.

"No one is perfect though, take that lady over there" I pointed to a lady in a hot, red two-piece made out of dental floss, "she may be flawless on the outside, but she might not be on the inside. Or, take that guy with the board" I said as I pointed to a man coming in from the ocean, "he might be fit and have fabulous hair, but maybe his home life sucks so he comes here to get away from it all." I added.

"You're probably right Kensie; it's just funny to watch some of these people lead lives that aren't their own. Sometimes I feel that way." Spencer said as he kept making buildings out of sand.

"Why do you feel that way?" I asked.

"I don't know; sometimes I just want to move back to Florida. I really miss my parents, and I want to see Eli.

"Who is Eli?" I said hoping he would actually answer a question without it being another question.

"When I was a sophomore, I became a big brother to this boy named Eli. His dad had passed away and his mom was a teacher at my high school. One of my coaches asked if anyone on our varsity team wanted to help the kid because he had been having some emotional problems." He said then stopped.

"How old was he?" I asked getting into a conversation we were going to finish if I had to make him.

"Seven. I told coach I would do it, so his mom paid me at first to take him places, we went and seen some exhibition baseball games, I took him to the park, out to eat, whatever. Then I got close to him, I took him everywhere I could. It got to where I told his mom I didn't want her money anymore. I did that until I was about 19. By then, Gabriel had already started college at USC; I was going to Florida State on a baseball scholarship. I still coached his baseball team in the summer. When I graduated, I moved to California. I have only been here about nine years." It just gets old being so busy all of the time." Spencer paused.

"That's very admirable of you. Do you talk to him often?" I immediately let Spencer's story find the soft spot in my heart.

"Yeah, he moved to Orlando, he's like twenty four now. He goes to college in Orlando, he's doing really well. I'd just like to see him face to face. I haven't seen him in about three years. Last time I visited mom and dad, he was in Colorado." He said as he stared directly at me. I was adding ages up in my head; that would make Spencer about 32- almost the same age as me and Gabriel. I think. He didn't really look that old, he had some early signs of eye wrinkles, and that laugh line from his beautiful smile, but if I'd have to have guessed, I'd said he was about twenty six.

"That's an awesome story Spencer. Do you realize how much you might have changed that boy's life? What we do in life somehow affects someone else's in some way." I said smiling.

"You're very theoretical, aren't you?" He laughed.

"Sometimes." I said still smiling, "What did you graduate with?" I asked.

"Majored in Public Relations, imagine that." He laughed.

"I will be so happy to have my journalism degree." I said back with seriousness.

"So, what do you do at the ad agency?" He asked.

"I pretty much bring in clients. Almost like the PR rep and I love doing that but some people can be pretty hard to work with." I said.

"I can imagine; I've seen it all." Spencer said as he smashed a building and started to recreate it.

"What have you been doing since you graduated?" I asked.

"Well, I started out writing screen plays, which I still do every now and then, but mostly I just play PR for Gabriel, so we are in the same kind of business." Spencer said harshly.

"Gabriel never mentioned you and he sure didn't tell me he knew you from Florida; probably didn't want me to know he had a PR Rep." I said while laughing. "Didn't you say you lived in Sarasota?" I asked as I rubbed coco butter lotion on my shoulders.

"Yeah, my parents live about a block and a half from Gabriel's, I supposed from your grandma too." He said taking his shirt off.

My jaw just about dropped off my face. I thought he was hot with clothes on, I never imagined he looked like that without a shirt on at all; the tank at the club did no justice to him without a shirt on. He had 4 tattoos on his arms; they were all tribal art, very nice, detailed tribal art. Up the back side of his left arm was a tattoo in tiny old English letters but I didn't know what it said.

"Nice tats." I said trying not to stare. "What does that say on the back of your arm?" I asked.

He extended his arm out straight behind him so I could read it. I got up to examine it closer.

"The Lord's Prayer, wow, whoever drew that had very crafty hands, very nice." I said as I let go of his arm and sat back down on my towel.

"Thanks, got any?" He probed as he looked at the spots on my body not covered by a suit.

"No, I was never brave enough to get a tattoo." I laughed.

"It's not that bad, you should get one while you are here." He laughed.

"I'm surprised I never seen you when I stayed with my grandma." I said changing the subject.

"I think I vaguely remember seeing you once or twice but it was probably years before she passed away. I didn't get off my block when I was younger. The neighborhood had some picnic at the park now and then but I didn't really hang out with Gabriel too much. It wasn't until we were in ninth grade that I started hanging out with him outside of school." Spencer looked up at me and smiled.

"It's weird we both knew him at the same time but didn't know each other." I smiled back. "I haven't been back to

Florida since my grandmother passed away." I said while looking down and moving the sand around with my bottle of lotion. "That was an important time for me. I got to do something most of my friends didn't, spend the summer away from home; away from everything. Since I now have kids, I wonder how my parents spent those few months every summer away from me; I couldn't imagine having time off from them." I said as I looked into the sky.

"Where's their dad? Is he not part of their lives?" Spencer probed as he finished up his sand castle.

I didn't know if I should help him or just watch him. His skin was so dark; his body just shinned on the beach. I was trying to coherently pay attention to our conversation and not stare at him. Oh yes, that's what they make sun glasses for! I dug mine out of my purse.

"You know, he really doesn't have much to do with them. I get some child support here and there, but for the most part, I don't want him around. He has no common sense what so ever. I guess I was blind when I met him, or on some re-bound from the last break up. I got pregnant with my oldest daughter not long after we met, and when we got married, I used his and my maiden name hyphened. When we got divorced, I just dropped his last name." I said without taking a breath.

"How long have you guys been divorced?" Spencer asked.

"Oh, about a year but physically we had been separated about two years before the divorce." I added.

"I'm not trying to go through all that crap" Spencer said with seriousness. "That's why I am never getting married. EVER. So, no boyfriend, recently divorced..." Spencer changed the subject.

"No, I told you I don't have the time. My oldest daughter, Rayanne, she is eight and she has some hyperactivity issues, besides the fact that she is just bad. She is very nosey and asks a hundred and one questions." I told him firmly as I flattened down on the towel on my stomach

"That's just kids" Spencer laughed. "Do they miss you?" He asked as he got up and sat next to me.

"They don't seem to notice I'm gone yet." I said with a smile.

"That's good; I mean, you don't have to worry. How old is the youngest one?" Spencer asked as he made a design with his foot in the sand.

Might I add that I hated feet, all feet. He had the most perfect male feet I had ever seen. His toes were really long, as were his fingers, but I guess if they were short, he would look funny since he was so tall. I tried so hard to figure out what was wrong with him.

"Marie is five. Do you have any kids?" I asked. Spencer got up and started getting water from the ocean to make a moat around his sand castle but he never stopped talking.

"I don't. I kind of avoided that. My parents argued a lot when I was growing up so I decided I wouldn't put my kids through that. I have watched Gabriel go through some shit with his ex over Ethan and I have managed to argue with every single girl I have ever liked so I don't." Spencer said.

"Don't what?" I asked as I sat up again. An alarm went off in my head...*that's what's wrong with him, he's a male whore. I should have known.* I thought to myself.

"Date for long periods of time, I just mingle." He said as he started laughing.

"Is that what you call it?" I laughed. "You looked like you didn't have an issue 'mingling' at the club" I said as I put up quotation marks around my words in the air.

"Yeah, that's what I call it, and I call this, a well-made sand castle." He said as he pointed to the sand. It was pretty cute.

"Gabriel and I tried to make sand castles when we were younger but they never held." I added.

"He still can't make them." Spencer said with half a smile.

"Got any pets?" I asked him.

"I don't. My apartment won't allow pets; I have a lab back home in Florida. He's going on 10 years old." Spencer said with sadness.

"I have a dog, Cairo, he's an Alaskan Husky, and I love him with my heart and soul. He's like the son I never had." I laughed.

"What's your favorite food?" He asked me with a goofy smile on his face.

"What is this, twenty questions? You writing a book?" I smiled.

"Maybe…" He still had that goofy look on his face, like he was up to something.

"Pizza." I said watching him with my eye brows scrunched because I knew he was up to something.

He grabbed the bucket he had been using, which was full of water, and dumped it on me; then ran off. It was cold. I wanted to continue half the conversations we started but I got up and chased him down the beach. He was quick. He was in the ocean before I knew it, and so was I. I started splashing him with whatever water my hands would hold; he just laughed at me.

He splashed me back and I tried to dunk him…that was a big mistake. I drank some salty ocean water. He grabbed me from behind and pinned me so I couldn't move. I was used to the water now; I tried to throw water behind me in his face but I was too tired to fight him. His arms seemed huge to me and I knew I was not getting out of the hold he had on my arms.

I paddled my feet while he held me, I was pressed against his chest and just watched the sky, I felt, I felt something. It was his aura, it blended with mine and I felt like it connected to form a circle around us. I wondered if the universe could see it, a magical bond.

All at once I thought; *this is so wrong*. We were probably in about twelve feet; I actually was about the same height as him. My head was directly next to his. There had to be something more wrong with him. He was so affectionate, he smelled good, he didn't have bad breath, there had to be something.

"You want to head back in? I have to check on my girls."
I used as an excuse for him to let me go so I could swim
back to shore.

"Yeah, I need to get back anyway." He said as he let go of
my arms.

As I swam back to the beach, I thought he was beside me;
but once I got out, he was behind me about five feet. He just
stopped; I couldn't tell if he was looking at me or something
else. The situation became awkward so I grabbed a towel
and walked to the edge of the beach.

"Did you want me to bring your towel to you sir, before
you left the water?" I said trying to make light of a really
messed up situation.

"Nope, just enjoying the view." Spencer said looking
directly at me, or behind me.

*Did he mean me? Did he mean the ocean, wait, the ocean
was behind him, what did he mean?* I started to analyze the
situation and I didn't want to. I promised myself I would
take this week out not to do that. Spencer came in from the
water and started to dry off. I went back into the water to
brush the sand off my legs and look at the sky again. It was
beautiful. I stood there for a while just looking at the
blue/grey sky that used to be over me in Tennessee. When I
turned around, he was sitting where I was sitting with his
shirt and shoes on, just looking forward.

I walked over to him, pulled my tank over my wet bathing
suit, and gathered up my towels.

"You okay?" I asked as I bent down beside him, hoping I
hadn't done something wrong.

"Yeah, I'm good; just thinking." He said as he stood up.

"Want to talk about it?" I said as I stood up beside him.

"Ever want to do something but you didn't do it because
you didn't know what the outcome would be?" He said as
he starting walking back towards the walk way.

"All the time-all the time." I said following him.

He never said another word. We waited on the Metro
Rapid to take us back; I was worn out. Neither of us said a

word during the ride. We got off at the coffee shop we met at.

"Do you want a ride back to the hotel, I'm going that way." Spencer asked.

"Sure." I said with a smile.

He opened my car door, again.

"You really don't have to do that; I kind of don't like it." I said as I got in.

Spencer shook his head and smiled as he shut my door.

"You should see the pier at night." He said as he reached for the volume button on the radio and drove off.

"I'd love to see it at night. I'd love to see a lot of things, during the day even." I said back humming the song that was on.

"Gabriel?" Spencer smiled.

"Not just him, other things too." I blushed.

Neither of us said anything else, I kind of felt bad for saying that, like I didn't have a good time or something. That sounded horrible.

"Thank you. I had a wonderful time today. I really did, and I appreciate you taking time out of your day to hang out with me." I said as I got out of the car, on my own, I didn't give him a chance to open the door.

"It was my pleasure, I hope to see you again soon, oh, hey, have fun tonight." Spencer smiled.

"Thank you." I smiled back as I shut the door.

I waved as I headed up the stairs to the hotel; I couldn't help but to look back at Spencer's car, *should I be looking at his car? What if he sees me? Oh well; do it any way* I thought to myself. I did, and he was looking back at me, then he waved. I didn't analyze his intentions; I just let it be what it was. I forgot to ask him what he got me.

Chapter 6-Gabriel

Gabriel called me at 7:30 p.m. and told me he would pick me up at 8; I was already ready. I made sure everything was perfect and I wasn't sure why-considering he had seen me at my worse. Of course, that was long ago but I wanted it to be perfect. I wasn't sure what kind of restaurant we were going to so I had on a simple black dress I wore to a funeral last year; it didn't really look like a funeral dress, more like an interview dress. It and the one Nora made me buy were the only two I had and I really didn't like the other one. I figured I'd take it back when I got home anyway. I pulled my hair up and Gabriel picked me up at 8:00 on the dot.

"I hope I'm dressed appropriately." I said as Gabriel kissed my cheek and opened my car door. *Should I tell him about the car door too? Nope, just going to leave that one alone;* I thought to myself.

"Its fine, you look great!" Gabriel said with a beautiful smile.

"Thank you, you look great too!" I said back. He had on nice button down shirt and tan pants. He didn't have the hat on so I actually got to see his hair. It was crew cut, shaved up the back with his bangs longer in front. I couldn't get away from those baby blue eyes. He had such a baby face and no facial hair what so ever.

"How was your day?" I asked politely.

"How was yours?" He asked back blankly.

"It was fine, I had a great day. Spencer is really sweet. We had a great time at the beach." I said with a strange look on my face. *Was he drilling me? Was I supposed to feel guilty for being with Spencer? Where was he going with this?* Just then it occurred to me, *was this Spencer's PR work? ME?*

"That's great; I'm glad you had a good time. The ocean is beautiful." Gabriel said as we drove off.

I started thinking again so it was silent between us, although it didn't take long to get to the restaurant. I was in deep thought, just because Gabriel couldn't spend time with me in a moment's notice, was he paying Spencer to entertain me? I began to become frustrated. *STOP*, I told myself, just stop trying to figure it out. Someone once told me not to analyze what I didn't know; but work on what I did know. What I knew was that I hadn't seen much of him, but he did pay for my vacation.

We pulled up to this nice restaurant and I was glad I chose the dress I was wearing. Gabriel was a complete gentleman, opened my door for me and helped me out of the car. I was a bit uncomfortable, I dealt with fancy people on a regular basis, but I was not fancy.

"So, how was your day?" I asked again after an uncomfortable moment of silence upon sitting at the table.

"It was okay, it's coming along, slowly. This screen play has been the slowest moving thing I have ever done. I'm glad you are having a great time, and I again, apologize for not making it to the beach earlier. I would have loved to have gone. Maybe in the next few days I can take you to the pier." Gabriel said in one breath.

The waiter came up and asked us what we wanted to drink. I ordered water; Gabriel got a scotch on the rocks, a bit strong for my tastes.

"Water? Do you want a glass of wine or a mixed drink?" Gabriel probed.

"I am still heat stroked from earlier so I am good with the water." I laughed.

"Do you have any set ideas about what you want to do while you are here?" Gabriel asked me.

"Not really. I want to see as much as I can. I have no idea when I can get back this way. Work has been kind of crazy lately." I said back with a smile as I rubbed the inside of my palms together.

"I wouldn't know." He chimed back.

"So, can you tell me what you are working on?" I asked seriously interested.

"It's a movie that is about to start filming at the end of the month. It's a comedy about these guys who take a trip around the world. There is a lot of filming in random places so everything has to be set up in advance." Gabriel said in his most adult mature voice.

"That sounds like it might be a bit confusing if you are going to be in different places all over." I said with excitement for him.

"It is, getting it all together but that's what pays my bills. So, in your email, you once told me if we were ever around each other again, you were going to tell me something important, here we are!" Gabriel switched from being mature to that fifteen year old boy I once knew.

"Wow, way to put some body on the spot. I don't know; it just doesn't seem appropriate." I said with a silly look on my face.

That put me on the spot, I wasn't ready to tell him I never stopped thinking about him, or that my world revolved around him, or that I compared every boy I ever met to him. I remembered I had a note in my purse that my therapist had me write when I was sixteen, *who am I kidding?* I knew it was there the whole time. I can't even remember why he made me write it or what we were talking about, but I won't ever forget what it said.

"So, I don't want to discuss business and I am going to force you to tell me what you wanted to tell me. Do you want to write it down? Like we did a long time ago? That was good stuff." Gabriel laughed.

"I still have those letters; it's funny because I never threw anything away. It's all at my parents, safely tucked away in a box in their basement." I said.

"You really kept all that stuff?" Gabriel beamed with light.

"I did. Maybe I could use them to black mail you with." I joked.

"Then I would have to trade something in return to keep you from black mailing me." Gabriel grinned, "I'm trying to think of something to talk about that we haven't already discussed through email." He added.

"Well, tell me about Ethan." I finally asked. It was silent for a while as he stared off across the restaurant.

"I don't get to see him as much as I want to. He stays with me a lot when I'm not working but I haven't seen him in the last few weeks. His mom is a real up tight bitch. She doesn't let him do anything. It's all about musical instruments and education, I commend her for that but he's just a kid. He's a good kid." Gabriel took out his wallet and showed me some recent pictures.

"Awe, he is really cute. He looks a lot like you when you were a boy." I said smiling. "At least you make an attempt to see him and spend time with him. That's the good thing." I added.

"That kid has everything he wants at my house. It just sucks that he doesn't get to be there as much as I'd like, his mom's a good mom, so I could never take him away from her, we just don't agree on anything. Hopefully things will unwind soon so he can stay with me more often." Gabriel was interrupted by the waiter asking if we were ready to order.

"What are you going to eat tonight K?" Gabriel asked me.

"I'm not sure yet, go ahead and I'll figure it out." I told him with a huge smile. He used to call me K. It made me feel really special that he remembered that.

"I'll have spaghetti marinara and extra garlic bread sticks, oh, and a salad with blue cheese dressing, thank you." Gabriel said as he passed the menu to the waiter.

"Yack! Blue Cheese?" I said and snarled my nose. "I actually would like to have the penne pasta." I told the waiter as I handed back the menu. "That actually sounds really good." I looked at Gabriel and smiled.

"Anyway, I told the ex that I would hire a nanny so he could go with me on some sets I was on last year so her rebuttal was to enroll him in some music school. He likes it so I wasn't going to fight her to keep him. Although, optimally, I would like to have him with me all the time, I know it isn't possible." Gabriel said as he put his wallet back into his pants pocket and placed his hand on top of the table.

"What happened between you and the ex?" I asked him.

"Well, we hadn't known each other long, I was producing my first movie and it wasn't something I planned. She was the lead in the movie and we split up before he was born. I was there when he was born, we had a paternity test done when he was six months, although I knew he was mine, and we just set visitation and child support at that point in time. She and I never got back together. She did let him stay with my parents for a few months last year and that was surprising." Gabriel grabbed my hand across the table and kissed it gently.

"Well, that's interesting, but at least you stayed by her side." I said with a smile.

"She loves money, she loves to be in the spot light, she put up her attempts to model in London, and it didn't work for her, although she is a beautiful girl." Gabriel let go of my hand and fiddled with his buttons on his shirt.

"He's a lucky boy to have you care for him. That doesn't always work out for some people." I said waiting for him to ask about my girls, in which he never did.

"Spencer and I have taken him to several Yankee games, I get great seats, and we try to do as much as we can with him, when he and I are alone, we play basketball and video games. He loves to read too, he's a smart little guy." Gabriel smiled again.

When our dinner came, we didn't say much. I didn't really know what to say. I was sitting with a man, who I had forever loved, the one that had my heart since I was five, the boy who I lost, then found, the guy I never gave up on and an adult best friend who never once asked about my life. I really was at a loss for words. It was almost like my life didn't exist. As soon as we finished eating, someone came up and asked for an autograph, in which he signed and they went on their way. It was an older lady; she was a fan of the sitcom the receptionist in my building was talking about. He politely thanked her, and then apologized to me. I told him it was no big deal, I didn't mind.

"Speaking of fans, my receptionist is a huge fan of yours; do you think you can sign something for her? I find it extremely hilarious." I said laughing.

"Sure, whatever you want. Why is that funny?" He said as he leaned back in his chair and put his hands behind his head.

"Asking you for an autograph." I smiled.

"You know there won't be a time you cannot call me directly and talk to me, ever, right?" He asked and smiled as he leaned forward.

"That's reassuring; I was worried about the autograph." I laughed.

"You're silly." He smiled. "I have something to show you!" Gabriel said with excitement.

"What is it?" I asked as he stood up.

"Just come with me…" Gabriel leaned over and grabbed my hand and led me to the side of the restaurant.

He opened a door and led me to a balcony that overlooked the city. It was beautiful. I could have never imagined the beauty of the city this late at night. The sky looked amazing. Gabriel grabbed my hands and spun me in a circle, then on the release, he didn't let go. I was standing in front of him over-looking the balcony and then up at the sky.

There was a lounge chair to the left of us, Gabriel led me over to it, sat down on it, and pulled me close to him. We were both facing forward and I was lying back on his chest.

We both watched the sky for a few minutes when he started to point out the big dipper and other stars. My heart was racing. I started remembering that boy I watched the stars with in my back yard, how I always wished Gabriel was there with me instead of him and now here he is, pointing out the cosmos…years later.

I had no idea what I was going to do. I had no idea if he expected me to sleep with him tonight, or go home; I began to think about all the years and times I thought about what I would do if I were in this position. I suddenly didn't know what to do. I was hot and cold at the same time. We stayed in that position for about an hour. Gabriel began to rub his fingers through my hair and down the back of my neck. I was a mess, mentally, I was so confused, *what should I say?*

He kissed the back of my neck, and then my shoulders and at once I decided to turn around to let him kiss me and bashed my head on his. He laughed, but that was just like me, to ruin a moment. If it could happen, it would happen to me, nothing good happens to me without repercussion.

Although he laughed it off, I know it hurt because it hurt me. He stood up and held out his hands, I put mine out, apologized for my malfunction, and he smiled and kissed me like he did when we were 15.

It lasted forever. It was passionate, caring, loving, and sensitive; all my emotions came rushing through me like fire.

"As much as I'd love to take you back to my house and do really bad things with you, I really have to get up early in the morning. I should probably be getting you back, if that's okay with you to call it a night?" Gabriel asked.

"That's fine, as much as I'd like to take you up on that offer, if it were the case, I probably better not." I said smiling but trying not to.

Did I do something wrong? I mean, I didn't want to sleep with him, I did but I didn't. My mind was telling me to remain calm about the situation, but my heart wanted him so badly. Our date lasted a little over two hours; I didn't want him to leave again. He took me back to the hotel and walked me up to my room and kissed me on the forehead.

"Goodnight, Kensie." He said smiling. "Thank you for a wonderful evening, I will call you tomorrow." He finished.

I put my hand up and slowly waved.

"Goodnight Gabriel," I said as I closed the door. I knew it was too late to call Nora, but I did anyway. She didn't answer, and I knew she wouldn't, but I left her a voice mail telling her to call me as soon as she got my message.

I sat in bed for what seemed like forever. I just couldn't sleep. I started drilling myself about how I could be so stupid to knock heads with him, like I was an infant learning to walk. *How could I have done that? I just ruined the night, or did I? What would I have done if he had invited me back to his place, or should I have invited him in?* I didn't know what to do. I wasn't that type of girl; one who just slept with people, but he wasn't just a person, he was my person-the person. Finally, about five in the morning, I fell asleep.

Chapter 7-Las Vegas

I woke up for some unknown reason that morning at 8:00. The sun was shining in my window. I looked out and seen the pool behind the hotel. I thought to myself, *this is my vacation; I should be enjoying it, not analyzing what everyone else is doing.*

I put on my swim suit from the day before, grabbed the book I had been reading on the plane and headed down stairs to the pool. There were kids playing everywhere, I decided to call my mom and talk to the girls, I missed them suddenly. No one answered. My mother refused to buy a cell phone. She said it isn't that important to have to talk to someone immediately.

I walked over to the vending machine and got a chocolate cupcake package and water, one heck of a breakfast. I found myself getting deeply into the book I was reading, escaping into some unknown fantasy world.

My phone rang, I thought it could be Nora, or my mom, or Spencer, or Gabriel, or Spencer, oh, I already thought that. He didn't even have my number, *who am I kidding?* I should have given it to him at the Pier in case Gabriel put him up to stalking me again. I kind of missed talking to him, he was really sweet. It wasn't anyone I wanted to talk to, my boss calling to see how my vacation was going and telling me I needed to be prepared when I came back for a really long week so relax now.

"You called me on vacation to tell me how busy I will be when I get back?" I said to him sharply but I wasn't surprised at all he called me.

I was on my stomach reading, my hair was pulled back in a bun-I am sure I looked pretty sexy. Even the people vacationing at the hotel were darker than I was. Sometime had gone by and I found myself re-reading what I had read because I could not focus. I looked up and I saw Josh standing at the gate. *What in the world is he doing here?* I thought to myself. Right behind him was Gabriel, with his hat, sunglasses, shorts, and a tank top. I put my head down, for what reason I had no idea, I wasn't ready for him to see me laid out like this, my stomach felt sick again, *what is wrong with me?* I thought to myself, *maybe he won't notice I'm over here. Oh, who am I kidding?*

So, I looked up, waved until they seen me, Gabriel pointed, as if to say, "There she is" as he hit Josh on the arm, then they came in the gate and walked over to me. Josh remained standing but Gabriel sat on the chair that was next to me, I didn't move.

Gabriel bent down to kiss me, in front of everyone. I thought that was odd. What if they knew who he was and then people started taking pictures or something then I would be on the cover of some gossip magazine looking like crap in my suit. A bit far-fetched but so be it. I kissed him back; it was just a short, sweet kiss.

"The receptionist thought she seen you come out here, or maybe you asking her how to get to the pool did you in. You can't hide from me." Gabriel said laughing.

"I was trying really hard to. How did you know?" I said back laughing.

"Did you get some sleep last night?" Gabriel asked.

"I think I fell asleep about five or so." I laughed.

"Why were you up so late?" He scrunched his eyebrows and asked.

"I was reading this book, it's pretty good." I replied as I looked down and realized I was only on page forty eight and I could have read that in about a half hour if I hadn't had to go back and reread everything because I wasn't paying attention to what I read when I read it.

"Have you talked to Spencer today?" He asked as he took my book from me and started thumbing through it.

"No, why would I?" I laughed.

"He was taking his car to be detailed and was going on a motorcycle ride and wanted your number to see if you wanted to go, I thought it would be a great idea." He said as he handed me back my book.

"I haven't heard from him." I said shaking my head.

Hum, why did that just happen? Why did I just think that I wished he would call? This kind of stuff doesn't happen to me, it's silly, I thought it, then it actually happened, but he didn't even call.

"I didn't know you were going swimming today, I should have called you earlier. I thought that might buy you some time before we leave." Gabriel smiled really big.

"Leave where? Where are you going?" I asked confused.

"Not just me, you too…" He said and stopped.

"Where are WE going?" I sat up and looked up at him taking off my sunglasses.

"Are you ready for this? I think you're going to be excited!" He kept smiling.

"Sure…" I said in my low tone voice thinking, *just tell me already!*

"We are going to Las Vegas baby!" Gabriel yelled out.

"Really?" I said back with excitement.

"We are going to a casino! I guess you will have time to get ready, so pack an overnight bag and I will pick you up at four and we will fly into Vegas. It will take about an hour. Don't eat anything big because we will have dinner when we get there, no more chocolate cupcakes." He said as he picked up the other one and took a bite of it. "Some things never change." He laughed.

"She was a sugar freak." He proceeded to tell Josh, "She ate chocolate like it was a meal when she was younger." He laughed.

"I don't do that so much now; it just sounded good this morning." I laughed back.

"See you at four." He said as he kissed my forehead.

I watched him walk away; he had the nicest back side. He stopped to talk to some people as he walked away, then waved at a couple and left the gate. A million things went through my head as he walked out that gate.
I knew I had to go shopping. I was determined to look my best for him.

I wondered if Spencer would be there. *Why was I wondering if Spencer would be there?* I took my hair out of the bun it was in and let it fall past my shoulders. I went back to my room and threw on a tank and some shorts. I headed down the strip and hit up every interesting store I could within a few blocks so I didn't get lost. I bought a long white dress and just knew it would go well with the white stilettos I had brought with me. I bought several post cards, shot glasses, and other memorabilia to take back home. That took a chunk out of my pocket. Suddenly, I was excited to be on vacation, instead of worrying about what was going to happen with Gabriel, I focused on Las Vegas, because I had always wanted to go there.

I decided to even out my burnt shoulders by getting a spray tan. I was so pale; I had to get dark quick. I did stop and grab some pastries at this little café; they looked so good from the window.

I went back to the hotel and stripped down to my bra and panties to admire the nice dark tan I just got. I washed my hair, but I pulled it right back up. I had yet to fix my hair and let it completely down. Well, I did take it out at the Pier but it was a mess. I decided to throw on a hat. I bought a White Sox hat just to get at Gabriel because I always liked the White Sox. I put on a pair of jeans, some flip flops, and a tank top, grabbed my bag that was never fully prepared for a trip and I went down stairs to wait at the door.

The bell boy was staring at me. He smiled, I smiled back. I wondered if he was looking at my chest, of course he was; *why wouldn't he?* I saw Gabriel's car at once and I thought he was going to get out, but Liam got out of the passenger side to come up to the building. I met him at the door and followed him to the car.

I wondered if the whole crew was going. When I got into the back seat, Josh was sitting on the left side. Liam closed the door for me and got back in the front seat. Gabriel was driving; he looked back and waved, smiled, and continued his conversation on his phone.

They were all really cute but this wasn't quite what I had in mind. I think Gabriel was on the phone the whole ride to the airport. I began to wonder where Spencer was and if he was coming. After about ten minutes of silence, Liam turned around and asked me if I was ready to do some gambling.

"Yeah, I have never been so it should be really cool." I said unexcitingly.

"You okay?" Liam said.

"Yes, I just miss my girls." I said with a smile at the big fat lie that just came out of my mouth.

Liam didn't say anything after that. It was quiet the rest of the way there. Gabriel was a pretty down to earth guy; he just seemed to be too busy for me at this moment. He seemed over whelmed in all the business he had going on. *Maybe I should have waited until he was done with this movie to come, but would I have ever?* So many things roamed my mind, but I tried to just enjoy being there. I waited for Gabriel to speak to me, but he didn't, not even a word about the White Sox hat.

It made me a bit uncomfortable. Josh never said two words to me and we sat next to each other the entire ride there. I decided that I was going to have a great night; I wasn't going to worry about what was actually happening. I was going to smile and be happy I was there.

When we got to the airport, I tried to make conversation with Gabriel, I offered to pay him for the plane ticket to Las Vegas, but he wouldn't take it. As we walked into the terminal, we got our tickets and around the corner walked Spencer in a tank top, shorts, black shoes, baseball hat, and he was carrying a duffle bag on his left side. I almost died when I saw him. Him just being him was superhot.

"We are going to stay at the casino's hotel, and fly back to LA in the morning." Gabriel finally said to me as we got on the plane. "Our rooms are right next to each other so you won't feel alone but you have your own room." Gabriel grinned.

On the plane it went, Spencer, me, Gabriel, Josh, then Liam in front of us. I'm not sure why they stuck me in the middle when they did nothing but talk over me the entire time about business.

I finally put my ear phones in and listened to some music to block them out. I had no desire to hear any bit of their conversation.

"What are you listening to?" Spencer muffled.

"What?" I said as I took out the ear plugs.

"What are you listening to?" Spencer repeated.

"Oh, just some random music, I listen to a lot of different stuff." I said back as I looked over and Gabriel was talking to Liam.

"That's cool, I'm pretty diverse myself." Spencer added.

"What's your favorite song?" I asked him as I turned my head to the left to look directly at him.

"I don't think I have one…maybe, I don't know." Spencer laughed. "You?" He asked.

"I don't know, I love classic rock. I don't think I have one either, maybe." I smiled at him.

When we landed and everyone gathered their stuff, Spencer disappeared. Liam and Josh never left Gabriel's side. We took a cab to the hotel, but Spencer didn't ride with us. After we got to the hotel, Gabriel waited a few minutes in the cab while Josh and Liam went in. I just sat there feeling uncomfortable again.

"Josh and Liam are getting our key cards, if you want to go in and grab yours, I won't be mad…" Gabriel laughed. It was almost like some high tech security move between them.

"I'm fine here, I can wait for you." I said as I looked down at my lap and twisted my hands around each other.

"I figured that we would go up to our rooms and meet in the lobby in an hour or two, then go have dinner at the restaurant; is that okay with you?" He asked politely.

"Yes, that's fine; it will give me a chance to change." I said as I looked up then back down again. He had to have sensed my sadness. I really didn't know why I was. I honestly felt like I was some body's little brother who was along for the ride. Some silence went by but I never looked up.

"What's up with the White Sox hat?" Gabriel said as he laughed suddenly.

I shrugged my shoulders that he noticed but I never changed the expression on my face.

"Did you do that to irritate me? I mean, I will buy you a Yankees hat if you want a good hat to wear." He laughed again.

"Oh, you noticed." I said sarcastically as I laughed. "I did buy it just to aggravate you, since I AM a White Sox fan, always have been, always will be...but, I'll take the Yankees hat." I laughed.

"Oh, come on; I noticed it as soon as you got in the car, if I hadn't been on the phone..." He paused like a light bulb popped in his head and he realized how shitty it was that he ignored me the whole time... "I would have made you take it off before you got in." He laughed as he pulled the front of my bill.

I felt bad; like I shouldn't show emotion of any sort, but at the same time, this ride I was on made me feel, emotionless. Josh and Liam returned with the key cards and we all walked in together. We rode the elevator to our floor and no one said a word. I stood there looking straight ahead when Gabriel pinched my butt. I just turned around and smacked him; he brought his arms in and laughed.

"This one is yours." He said as he opened the door for me. "Meet in about an hour or so at the restaurant?" Gabriel asked me.

"Yeah-Yeah." I said as I threw my hands in the air and walked into the room shutting the door behind me. I never looked back.

I so wanted to take a nap when I saw that huge bed. I was so tired but I sat on the edge of the bed looking around at the room. It was nice. All neutral colors, nice dim lighting, and a Jacuzzi in the bathroom. I started to unload my bag, laying everything out on the bed and staring at it. I looked out the window and stared into the city. The window had a small seat so I sat down and watched the sky for a while. After deciding I had enough self-worth thoughts, I started putting on my makeup, to which I had barely put any on the entire time I was in California.

I brushed my hair out and used the curling iron hanging on a slot in the bathroom to curl the ends. They had brand name shampoo and soap; it was a very nice hotel room. I stood in the mirror and looked at myself for about twenty minutes. I realized when I looked at my phone that it had been two and a half hours since I had been in there.

The time went by way too fast. I'm not sure if I was fighting with myself over if I wanted to do this anymore or if I was just battled old demons. I looked at myself again and shrugged my shoulders. I walked out of my room and headed towards the elevator. I pressed the button and as I stepped in…

"Hold that door!" Someone yelled. I put my hand in the door to keep it from closing.

In walked Spencer. We had to stop meeting like that, and *where did he come from anyway?* He didn't even ride with us to the hotel. Liam was right behind him, they both looked really nice. Spencer had on nice button up, long sleeved shirt, a pair of tan pants, and brown dress shoes.

"Wow Kensie, that dress is hot." Spencer said as he was checking me out.

"Thanks, you look hot yourself, Spencer." I said back blushing.

Liam laughed and stood next to me. I took pride in myself and I knew I wasn't ugly, but people telling me I was beautiful didn't really feed my ego, I just smiled and put my head down. The entire ride down the elevator, I kept my head down, staring at Spencer's shoes. I have no idea why, I think it was because I knew he was beside me checking me out. I was embarrassed but excited at the same time.

When we stopped, I let them go out first. I was sure they knew where we were going so I let them lead. I stayed behind them until we were inside. Gabriel was seated at a table and he had on a suit; black jacket, white shirt, black tie. There were 3 really big guys standing behind him in suits. I knew I looked good, I spent two hours on myself; I was confident but, scared and intimidated.

My hair was down, curled on the ends, bangs swept to the right side, I had on my white stilettos, and this dress, it was something I would never part with. It was open in the back, had a slit down the side, came down in the front to a "V" and was long. Sheer, off-white; beautiful. I am not a modest person in any way, but I knew this dress was hot.

I think I spotted Gabriel before he noticed me. He looked up at me, had a blank look on his face then stood up and apparently his belt got caught on the table because he knocked the chair over. I will NEVER forget the look on his face. I just laughed.

"I really don't know what to say Kensie, but WOW!" Gabriel laughed.

"Thank you, you look, wonderful! I have never seen you this dressed up before." I said as I sat down at the table and Gabriel pushed my chair in.

"Thank you, that dress is absolutely beautiful."

They ordered appetizers, three samplers of mozzarella sticks, stuffed mushrooms, calamari, and onion rings. Gross. I took a mozzarella stick and called it that. We all started to make acute conversation and NO ONE, I mean NO ONE, brought up business. That was nice. I ended up ordering a salad.

Gabriel and Spencer both sat across from me and they both kept staring at me. I was torn between who to look at and who to smile at. I just smiled and laughed at everything they said but in reality, I wasn't really paying much attention to any of it.

After we were finished eating, Spencer wanted to get a picture of us. He handed his phone to one of the bigger guys and he took a picture of Gabriel, Spencer, and I. After we took the picture, we all went into the casino. It was quite a group. I felt a bit strange, not used to having huge guys standing around me but I suppose Gabriel needed that to feel safe. He asked me to join him at the Poker table. I didn't know much about Poker, or gambling. I just sat next to him for the next few hours watching him win some, and loose some. He passed money out like I have never seen anyone do. He had more money than I had made my entire life. I was really happy for him to have accomplished so much in his life; I just started to get bored.

I tried to play with him; he tried to teach me how to play. I lost most of the money I brought with me so I told him I was going to play craps because it sounded interesting. Gabriel stood up and kissed my forehead then sat back down to finish his hand. As I stood up, Gabriel motioned to Spencer towards me; I guess he was supposed to baby sit.

I went to the craps table and started throwing my dice. It was actually a lot of fun; however, I never won. Spencer stood beside me but never said a word. Not ONE word. I really have horrible luck, luck plays favorites, and I'm not one of them. I lost every bit of the money I brought down stairs except for ten bucks.

"I'm done." I finally said as I turned around to see if Spencer was still standing there.

"Want to go have a drink at the bar?" Spencer said as he pointed behind him.

"I'm broke." I laughed.

"I got this." Spencer said as he put his hand on the middle of my back and led me to the bar.

"You haven't said much the entire evening, everything okay?" Spencer asked me as we sat down at two bar stools.

"Yes." I hesitated to say.

"You aren't having a good time." He said with a half-hearted smile.

"Oh, I am. This is great. I have not done half the things in the last year that I have done in the last two days." I began. "I'm very happy for Gabriel; I guess I just expected to actually see him more. Maybe for him to pay attention to me a bit more." I continued.

We both ordered a drink and I could see him staring at me through my peripheral vision.

"One day, you will be so happy; you won't know what to do with yourself." He said with a positive attitude, "What do you want out of life, I mean, what are your goals?" He asked as he took a drink.

"I don't think I know, I want to write, I want to see the ocean every day, now that I have seen it again, I want to be around it every day. I used to want to move to New York, but I don't know. Maybe I will move to Florida. I want my girls to have every opportunity to have more than I ever did and every opportunity to do it. It's all about money, if you have it, you're good, if you don't, you are screwed." I said then stopped for a second, "If I want to fly to Paris, I should be able to do that." I finished.

"Never been…" Spencer said and stopped. "To Paris that is. If I hadn't come here with Gabriel, I would probably be coaching some kids' baseball team in Florida still doing nothing, pretty much what I do now. Why did you want to move to New York? Ever been there?" Spencer asked.

"Yeah, on my senior year spring break. I loved it. Have you ever been?" I asked picking up my drink.

"Many, many times. I've been all over. Not too much out of the US, but I've been to Maine, New York, New Jersey, everywhere. Boston was my favorite." He said back smiling. "Why don't you move here? There are so many writing jobs and you can see the ocean every day." Spencer said turning his stool towards me.

"Well, that would be a big jump; a little farther than I would like to be-away from my parents. I'm not sure I could leave them like that." I said.

"Well, if you want to think about it when you get home, I'm sure we all could help you in any way you might need, anything, ever, at all." Spencer said seriously.

I didn't say anything, I contemplated my thoughts and entertained the idea, as I sat there staring at my drink. I should be having fun right now, I haven't been away from my girls like this ever and I was wasting it away worrying about next week and what I should or shouldn't do.

"Can I ask you a question?" I turned towards Spencer with one leg in front of me and the other on the side facing him.

"Sure." Spencer said as he took a drink of his beer.

"Am I your PR work? I mean, it seems like if Gabriel doesn't have time to spend with me, you have been here and we have abruptly ran into each other at random times. I was just curious if he pays you to hang out with me." I said as I looked down at my drink.

"I would NEVER let him pay me to hang out with you. I like you, a lot; you are really laid back and wonderful to be around. That was never an intention. He never really asked me to hang out with you. He never said anything until tonight when you left the Poker table. He may have just been concerned with you roaming around by yourself. But, the truth…" Spencer leaned in to my ear with his beer in his hand… "I was going to go with you anyway." He smiled.

"Thank you, you are really sweet Spencer. I really had a great time at the pier the other day." I smiled.

"You know, they have a night club in here some place, we could go listen to some music, you could dance or something." Spencer said.

"Sure, I have spent enough money for one evening." I laughed as I stood up.

Spencer and I went into the night club and they were doing karaoke. Spencer got us both a drink and we sat at a dimly lit table in the back. I felt weird but hell, I realized you only live once and I had more conversations with Spencer than I did Gabriel anyway.

"You sing?" I asked Spencer.

"Only in the shower." He laughed.

"I love to sing, but only to myself." I laughed with him as I yelled over the person singing.

"You should do it." He said pointing to the stage.

"I am not singing." I laughed.

Spencer got up and walked over to the DJ who had a list of all the songs you could do to Karaoke. There was a younger guy up there looking through the books. I almost died because I knew what he was doing. Spencer sat back down at the table.

"What did you do?" I asked him.

"Told that guy you wanted to sing a song and he gave me these for you to look at." Spencer said as he popped some pages out on the table.

"Oh, no you didn't." I blushed and laughed.

"I did, so pick one. I want to hear you sing." Spencer said.

So I sat there for a few minutes staring at the cover page, then I wondered what songs were on there. The younger guy who was up there got up to sing. I knew the song as soon as the music came on. '*Little girl tonight baby don't be blue dig those pretty lights along the avenue...*' He was singing "Boardwalk Angel" by John Cafferty. He sounded a lot like him; I couldn't help but watch him intently. Spencer stared at me the whole time; I could feel him staring at me.

"You never told me what your favorite movie is." He smiled at me as I turned to look toward him.

"I don't have one, I told you that." I smiled at him and shook my head.

"I will tell you mine after you tell me yours." He laughed looking ahead at the younger guy singing.

"Shush! I'm trying to listen to him sing!" I blurted out and smiled.

'*This world has let you down; and broke your heart, but tonight's the night for a brand new start, leave this world behind...*' the younger guy was singing and I was intently watching him.

Spencer just smiled back and turned his head towards the guy singing, then back at me. I could see him looking at me as I watched. This guy was good.

'*So meet me out on the Boardwalk tonight, meet me down by the sea*'…The song was almost perfect. Spencer kept staring and I kind of wanted him to stop because it made me self-conscious. I started thumbing through the pages, ordered another drink, sucked it down, and thumbed through the pages some more; then I stood up, marched my ass up to the DJ and told him I wanted to sing. He penciled in my song then a lady got up to do a song; I had no idea what it was. We both looked each other and laughed. She sounded horrible.

When she was finished singing, the DJ looked at me and nodded. I was half buzzed by now anyway so I was feeling pretty good. I stood up and started to walk up to the stage. I should have tripped. I know if it had been a regular day, I would have. I turned around half way to see what Spencer was doing and he was smiling at me, cheering me on. I just smiled and grabbed the microphone.

I chose Bonnie Tyler's "*Total Eclipse of the Heart.*" I don't know why, but it sounded good to me. I was shy in the beginning, I didn't let it loose until the chorus came in, and Spencer just stared at me, holding his beer. As I belted out '*Every now and then I fall apart, and I need you now tonight*' Spencer sat his drink down.

Everyone in the place was staring at me. I was nervous but I let it rip. It got really quiet in there and it made me nervous but I really was pretty toasted. My vocal cords cooperated with me and I could hear myself echo. It actually sounded pretty decent in the night club. As I sang '*I really need you tonight, forever's going to start tonight,*' Spencer got up and moved to a table closer to me. As I continued, '*Once upon a time I was falling in love, now I'm only falling apart…*' He made me incredibly nervous because he sat in the chair away from the table with his elbows on his knees staring right at me. I sang with every bone in me shaking, I looked at Spencer a couple of times after that but I didn't want him to think I was singing it to him, but I might have been.

When I finished, everyone clapped. Even the boy who did "Boardwalk Angel" patted me on the back. I shook his hand as I sat at the table that Spencer ended up at and he looked dumbfounded.

"You have an awesome voice Kensie, that song was made for you, I swear it was." He said as he turned in towards me.

"Okay, I sang, now you have to dance with me." I smiled.

"I told you I don't dance." He laughed.

"That is NOT fair." I laughed back.

"I hate to dance. No phobia, I just hate it." He said but never gave me an explanation of why.

As I readjusted my legs under the table, I brushed his leg with my mine. He didn't move his leg. He kept watching the person singing but never moved. I moved my leg and then he stretched his leg out to touch mine again. I didn't move this time. We sat there and listened to a few other people sing, they were pretty good too. This one guy had an amazing voice. We talked about the club, how cool it was, the casino, the fancy soap and shampoo in the rooms. Another hour had passed.

"I think I'm going to head to my room, I'm really tired, and slightly drunk." I finally said.

"Would you like me to walk you?" Spencer asked as he stood up when I did.

"No, I'm fine, I can find my way back, but thank you!" I smiled.

Spencer leaned in and kissed my cheek and said goodnight as he followed me out the door and back towards the casino. I got on the elevator headed upstairs and realized I left my purse at the original table we were at. I was freaking out. I couldn't get in my room without my key card, my phone, everything was in there. Leaving things behind seemed to be an ongoing problem for me.

So I headed down the elevator back to the night club and I saw Gabriel, Spencer, and everyone else coming towards me. I jumped behind the wall so they didn't see me.

"Why did she go back to her room?" Gabriel was asking Spencer in mid conversation.

"She said she was tired and I know she spent most of her money." Spencer replied as he pressed the elevator button up.

"Why didn't you give her some? She could have found me; I would have given her some money." Gabriel was telling Spencer.

"I don't know, I don't think she would have taken it; besides we went to the night club, she sang, man, that girl has a set of pipes on her." Spencer told Gabriel as he stood there with his hands on his hips smiling.

"Did you go upstairs with her?" Gabriel asked.

"WHAT? She went by herself. Exactly what are you saying Gabriel?" Spencer sounded angry.

"I don't know-it just seems like you have spent more time with her than I have." Gabriel said in a calm voice.

"Maybe you should spend more time with her than me; she is a really sweet person." The elevator door opened and they got on and I couldn't hear any more of their conversation.

I went to the club and thankfully, my purse was still there. Kind of ironic I left my purse and heard the conversation Gabriel and Spencer had about me. I have no idea why I hid. I just didn't want to deal with either one of them.

As soon as I got back to my room, I took full advantage of the bathtub and passed out on my big, fluffy bed.

I woke up at 7:00 in the morning. I guess my body was programmed to do that no matter how little sleep I had. I think I had adjusted to their time zone. I looked around the room and something looked different. There were fifteen red roses on the dresser. *Were they from Gabriel or from Spencer?* I didn't know, I was confused. *Was I there to spend time with my long lost friend or make a new one all over?* I didn't usually let people get close to me, but I was growing attached to Spencer in some way I couldn't explain.

I picked the gorgeous dress I wore up off the floor and put it in my bag. I started packing my things and put on some shorts and a tee shirt. My cell phone rang, it was Gabriel.

"Did you get the roses?"

"Yes, they are beautiful." I said with a smile.

"One for every year we didn't know each other." He said.

"Awe, that is so sweet!" I exclaimed. "How in the world did you get in here? How did you do that without waking me up?" I asked.

"I have my ways, and why didn't you tell me you needed money last night?" He asked.

"It isn't your job to give me money. I have money; I just didn't want to blow it all. I had self-control." I said laughing.

"I'm sorry I spent most of the evening in the casino and that you had to spend most of the evening with Spencer..." Gabriel said but I cut him off...

"It was fine, I had a great time." I replied mid-sentence.

"To make it up, I am hoping when we get back you will go with me to take Ethan to Six Flags and then instead of staying at the hotel, you would stay with me at my house tonight?" Gabriel asked but said.

"That sounds cool, how will he react to my being there?" I asked knowing my girls would flip out if some guy came home with me.

"He's six, he'll be fine, trust me." He said. "It will just be us" Gabriel finished.

"That's fine." I said in a daze. I was either still hung over or was unsure of meeting Ethan, or going with Gabriel to begin with.

"If you aren't up for it, we don't have to go." Gabriel said with sadness in his voice.

"I'm fine with it, Gabriel, I really would like to go. I think I'm just not quite with it yet. I had a lot to drink last night." I said back trying to be more active in the conversation.

"Great! I really want you to meet him and I think you will love it." Gabriel said back with a happy tone. "I will see you soon, we will be leaving in a few hours. Are you hungry?" Gabriel asked.

"No, not really. I'm going to get myself together but thank you!" I said back as I wiped my make up off my face.

"Well, miss K, I will see you soon!" Gabriel finished.

I stood there looking at my roses, looking at the room, looking out the window then began to gather up all my things. I tried to tuck the roses in my bag but I let them hang out of the top to get air. I found myself in the lobby waiting on everyone to come downstairs; I knew I was leaving this beautiful hotel with nothing but empty thoughts.

Chapter 8-My Dream

When we got on the plane, I sat in between Gabriel and Spencer again. I decided I needed to call mom and Nora when I got back to the hotel. This was strange for me and I needed some advice. Gabriel tried to make conversation.

"Hey, do you remember that time we went swimming with your dad and that 350 plus pound guy stood up and had on a purple Speedo?" Gabriel asked me.

"I could never forget that, I was traumatized." I said

"YOU were traumatized?" Gabriel laughed.

"That was the best memory of that summer." I added.

"What kind of writing are you trying to do?" Gabriel asked me like he needed something to talk about.

"I don't know, just playing around with some journalism right now. I want to work for a newspaper, I guess." I said as I noticed Spencer asleep with his head tipped back and his hat over his face.

"If you do any novel writing, write some stuff down for me and what you can't come up with, I can get a ghost writer to finish. We could work on a manuscript together and I can propose it to some people and see if we can get it sent to production. I can pitch it to some directors and see where it goes." Gabriel was completely enthusiastic.

"I can try. It's just been difficult to think about writing on my own with the girls, work, and school." I said.

"When you get home, think about it and let me know, after this movie is done, I will have some time off." Gabriel said as he grabbed my hand and squeezed it. He held my hand the rest of the plane flight and gently rubbed the outside of my thumb…all of a sudden; butterflies. It almost felt surreal for some reason. When we landed, Gabriel never left my side, I had Gabriel on one side, Spencer on the other until we left the terminal and Spencer disappeared again. Gabriel had Liam drive us back to the hotel and he sat in the back seat with me, he leaned his head over to my shoulder, I rubbed the inside of his face and roughly five minutes later, he was asleep.

I didn't stop rubbing his face, I wanted to take a nap with him, I wanted to wake up next to him, but for some reason, it just didn't feel right anymore, it's like something I wanted for so long suddenly changed.

We got back to the hotel pretty early. I had little time to unpack my things and get ready to go again. It was going to be about a forty minute drive to Valencia-to Six Flags, and I had roughly an hour to make my phone calls.

"Hello mom, how are the girls?" I asked as soon as my mother answered the phone.

"They are good; your dad took them to the park. They are so funny; Rayanne is so full of questions. She asked the lady at the ice cream parlor why her feet were so big yesterday, it was rather embarrassing." My mother said.

"Who honestly calls it an ice cream parlor anymore?" I laughed.

"How are things going dear, are you having a good time?" She asked and waited for an answer.

"I am. Spencer has been really busy." I said without thinking.

"Who is Spencer?" My mother asked while I collected my thoughts.

"Did I say Spencer? I meant Gabriel. He has been working on this screen play and has been busy. We just got back from Vegas, we went to a casino." I said quickly changing the subject.

"That sounds like fun, once again, who is Spencer?" My mother asked.

"He's Gabriel's PR rep, he's wonderful, I mean, I have spent a lot more time with him than I have Gabriel. They were friends in Florida. He lived a block or so away from grandma but I had never met him." I said.

"Oh, he went with Gabriel to California?" My mother asked giving me her motherly duty.

"Yes, well, eventually he did; he's been pretty cool. He's a really nice guy; all his friends are very nice, but Spencer is super tall." I added.

"Hum." My mom said and stopped. That's good Kensie; I will tell the girls you love them when they get back." She said.

"Thanks mom, love you and tell dad I love him too and I will call tomorrow." I finished.

I didn't have time to call Nora but I made a mental note that I needed to do that when I got back. Gabriel and Ethan picked me up shortly after that and I wanted to swallow Ethan whole. He was the cutest little thing, he didn't really look a lot like Gabriel in person, but I could see definite facial features that were the same.

He welcomed me with an open heart and offered to share his gummy bears with me. He was so quiet on the ride there. It was just the three of us and finally, some conversation with Gabriel, alone.

"So, this place is huge, and I will warn you, Ethan will want to go on all the rides he can." Gabriel informed me.

"I have always wanted to go but never got the chance. My ex and I were going to take the girls to an amusement park once but it never happened. Marie was too young at the time." I said.

"It's a lot of fun no matter how old you are." Gabriel noted. "How are your girls doing?" He finally asked. Trumpets sounded in my head, FINALLY, finally he asks me about my girls.

"I haven't talked to them too much at all. My mom and dad have kept them busy. Every time I talk to them, they are ready to get off the phone." I replied.

I guess being around Ethan made Gabriel realize that there is a life outside of this screen play and some people do have children they still think about. I'm surprised he finally asked about them.

"I bet they are having a great time. Your parents were always really cool with kids." He smiled as we went into the amusement park.

"Yeah, they did a bang up job here." I laughed.

"You turned out fine." He smiled.

"Just to let you know, Liam will be following us around while we are here, for security reasons, but normally, I don't get noticed unless I don't have my hat on, and of course, I'm in a suit. People don't recognize me too often when I am in basketball shorts." He said shortly. I looked around for Liam as we pulled into the parking lot but I didn't see him.

"I was wondering about your security issue." I said as I continued to see if I could spot him.

As soon as we got there, we found the fun house; we stopped at the mirrors to make goofy faces. It was like we were 10 again hiding from each other like we did at the county fair. We played some games; Gabriel had an arm on him. He won a huge bear playing basketball, in which he had the guy hold until we got ready to leave.

"Daddy, look at this!" Ethan yelled as we were walking towards some vendors.

"Those are cool." Gabriel said as he took some huge, fat sunglasses down from the dispenser.

"Can I have em?" Ethan asked as Gabriel put them on his face.

"Sure, I think we will get some too." Gabriel replied as he put some purple ones on me. I just laughed.

We walked around the amusement park with these goofy huge glasses on the rest of the day.

"What's so funny?" Gabriel asked me as I laughed.

"You look like a bug." I laughed hysterically as I pushed the glasses farther down my nose and looked over them.

"You look like a big ant." He laughed back.

"You look like a tiny head alien with big eyes." I said as he pushed my sunglasses back against my face.

I locked arms with Gabriel on his left side as he held on to Ethan's hand. We took Ethan to some smaller roller coasters. I started to think about how calm a boy is. Compared to my girls, he was an angel. He went round and round and just waved at us. My arms were still locked with Gabriel's but he now had his right hand on top of mine. He squeezed my hand tightly and looked down at me and smiled.

I wished my girls could have been there, but in the back of my mind, I knew I would be too frustrated to enjoy the day. I started thinking about how great it would be if Ethan had been our boy, not that I didn't love my girls, but how things might have turned out different if my grandma hadn't passed away. Gabriel was a wonderful dad. I wished I could still love him, but I knew in my heart, I didn't know him anymore. He was and wasn't the same person.

As Ethan rode all of the kid rides; and we stood by and watched, making minor conversation. When he seemed to be wearing down, we decided to get something to eat. I got a hot dog and some ice cream.

"Remember the last year we went to the county fair?" Gabriel said out of the blue.

"Yeah, we got stuck on the Ferris wheel for twenty minutes at the top because of some malfunction they were having." I laughed.

"No, not that, remember when we were talking about going before we went and you said you wanted caramel apples and an elephant ear?" He stared directly at me.

"Yeah, I think so; I remember eating it if that's what you are asking me." I laughed trying to anticipate where this was going.

"I had to mow five yards that day and take out an advanced allowance to pay for that stuff. It's so funny that here we are years later and I could now fly you anywhere you wanted to go, if you asked me." He laughed.

"You didn't tell me that. You did pay for everything that day; I spent the money my mom gave me on a poster at the music store the next day." I laughed wondering why he was still staring directly at me.

"I loved you so much Kensie, it broke my heart when you left." He said seriously but never looked away from me.

"I, I, never knew that, I mean, I guess I knew that you were my best friend, and I..." I couldn't find the words. They escaped me, my words I had recited in my mind over and over and over had flown away. "I loved you with all my heart." I finally said looking down but I realized I didn't want to have this conversation with Ethan there.

Ethan never said a word. He just kept eating his chicken fingers looking around at everything.

"I hope that our children never have to endure what we went through. It was rough. I stopped playing basketball for a while. Come summer the next year, I never went outside." He said but never took his eyes off me.

I began to get teary eyed. I really was at a loss for words. I couldn't stare him directly in the face because it made me uncomfortable to have to look at his beautiful blue eyes and feel. I guess I decided I didn't want to feel anymore.

"It definitely changed me, it's almost like the loss of my grandmother didn't affect me as much as it did loosing you; like it masked the pain so I had something else to think about. It didn't hit me my grandma had passed until the next summer." I said as I let a single tear run down my face.

Gabriel stood up from the table and walked over to me, bent down on his knees and wiped the tear away.

"I really, really am sorry, K, for everything." He smiled.

I smiled back and rested my head on top of his.

"Daddy?" Ethan had gotten up and tugged on Gabriel's shirt. "Can we go over there?" Ethan said as he pointed to the bumper cars.

"We can talk more, later?" Gabriel said as he looked up at me with his big beautiful smile.

"Yes, I'd love that." I smiled back.

We spent the rest of the afternoon riding rides we all could get on; when we walked to each ride, Gabriel held my hand warmly, with those goofy glasses on. We had a really good day but we didn't stay real long. I wished my girls could have gone.

We got back to Gabriel's house about 9:30. When we pulled up, he put in a password at the gate that guarded his house. The drive way wasn't too long. There were tall white pillars in the front and fancy hedges and bushes around the front of the house. My parent's had a decent house, however; mine was far from this extravagant. No one I knew had a gate that required a password. I expected someone to come out and park his car, or open the door, but no one did.

I wondered if that was what he was used to, someone always doing things for him. I had hoped there weren't any maids because that was a bit too deep for me. I looked to the side of the house and there was a window about 30 feet tall on the side. You could see a staircase going up the side. The house was amazing.

He opened the door like a normal person and turned off the alarm as we went in. He told Ethan it was time for bed as we walked in the door. His house was immaculate. It wasn't spotless, which humored me, and I saw no sign of maids. There were basketballs and footballs on the floor, and a box of cars in the middle of the hall way. It was way too big and too little of anything else. Certain areas looked like no one even lived there.

"If you want to wait for me in the living room," Gabriel pointed to the left, "I will put Ethan in bed and be back down in a few minutes." Gabriel said while walking up the stairs.

"Goodnight." Ethan said.

He was so incredibly adorable. I sat on the couch and noticed that Gabriel had a taste for paintings. I saw one I recognized and got up to look at it above the fireplace. It was huge. Gabriel had pictures of Ethan everywhere. I didn't want to be nosey so I sat back down on the couch, almost afraid to touch anything. The floor was marble and there was a beautifully woven rug in front of the couch.

For some reason, I started wondering what Spencer was doing. *What did he do on his days off from Gabriel?* I thought to myself and chuckled.

"So, what do you want to do tonight? You will have me all to yourself." Gabriel said as he came into the living room and shut off his cell phone. "We can watch some movies, we can swim, hot tub, whatever you want to do. Do you still like to play pool? We can see how bad you are at it, improved any over the years?" Gabriel asked.

"Actually, the slop I played when we were fourteen is nothing like now; I actually love to play pool. The last time we played pool together was on your dad's pool table and I hardly think we understood the game." I laughed.

"Okay, well then K, follow me and we will see what you are made of." Gabriel laughed while grabbing my hand and leading me to a set of stairs.

We went into his basement and there was a dart board, a pool table and tons of reclining chairs with several flat screen televisions. Gabriel turned on some music and I got myself into position to kick his ass.

"I don't think you can distract me miss, so that pose you are making isn't going to help you win." Gabriel tried to ignore me.

"What pose? This is how I stand." I laughed.

I don't think he knew what he was in for. I actually could play some pool. I took my shot and turned around, he was right behind me. We bumped into each other, but this time it wasn't my fault. My head touched his chest; he bent down and kissed me. Every time he touched me, I melted.

Needless to say, I beat him in pool. I began thinking to myself, someone wake me from this dream. After we finished a few games of pool, he gave me a short tour of the house and we went back to the living room area. I call it area because I think he had two or three living rooms. This house was huge. We sat down on the couch and it was really weird for me. We were about two people apart and he would scoot over away from me, and then scoot back towards me. I just looked at him.

He repeated this for about a half hour or so, laughing at me. I finally busted out in laughter and poked him in the chest. Eventually we met in the middle and ended up watching some scary movie. It was getting late and I could tell he was drained.

"I'm glad you're here." He said as he began to lay down behind me.

He wrapped his arm around my waist and pulled me down in front of him. He put his other hand above his head and kissed my neck. He started twirling my hair above my head.

"I'm glad I'm here too." I said as I pulled his hand to my face and gently kissed the inside of his palm.

I turned towards him as he hit the light, all I could hear is the huge grandfather clock ticking in the corner. It was pitch black. He grabbed the blanket from behind him and covered me up with it. I put my head on his stomach and a single tear ran down my face. I think he fell asleep before I could even let the tear hit his shirt. I tried to wipe it away before he noticed. I was happy to be there. If this was what it felt like to truly love, I wanted it to last forever.

That was it, sleep. I have nothing exciting to report, but for me, it was wonderful to have someone hold me. I can't remember the last time that happened. I didn't search for his heart beat; I fell asleep before I could remember I wanted to listen to it.

Ethan woke us up at 9:30, I was lying on my side and Gabriel was on his back when I woke up. At least he wasn't snoring.

"Shit, what time is it?" Gabriel said as he jumped over me to grab his phone.

"It's 9:30." I said as I sat up looking at my phone half awake.

"I have a meeting this morning and I have to drop Ethan off before 11!" He exclaimed.

"I'm sorry, if I had known, I would have set my alarm on my phone." I said apologetically

"Do you want some breakfast? I can make you something, I have plenty of time." He offered once he realized my feelings were a bit hurt.

"I'm not hungry but thanks for asking." I told him as I put my shoes back on.

"I know I will be tied up all day but maybe later this evening we could go to the Santa Monica Playhouse of performing arts." He said as he turned his cell phone back on.

"That sounds wonderful, just call me and let me know so I can cancel my plans." I laughed.

"Sometimes I hate the fact that I own one of these." Gabriel said with disgust as his phone beeped about fifteen times.

"I can't get anyone to call me." I laughed.

Gabriel dialed someone's number while he was getting milk for Ethan's cereal.

"What's up?" Gabriel said, "Yeah, I just got up. I have to take Ethan home and get to that meeting, you still going?" Gabriel said and paused.

Gabriel stepped outside the kitchen and I started looking for the spoons. Ethan pointed to the drawer they were in and I handed him his breakfast. I could hear Gabriel muffled but I think I heard what he said.

"Yeah, we had a good time. Not enough hours in a day." He paused. "What? He said as he laughed. "So what if I did; but I didn't" He finished.

He started to head down the hallway as he said, "You got a crush on her don't you?" Then he laughed.

I couldn't hear any more of the conversation, I sat with Ethan while he ate, and we talked about music school and how he can't understand the notes on the piano.

"Uncle Spencer can play the guitar." He offered as we started talking about musical instruments.

"He can? I didn't know that. Maybe you should ask him to teach you how to play." I said back in astonishment.

"He taught me some stuff, I don't remember it though."
He smiled back at me.

I brushed his hair down and fixed his collar on his shirt.
He just smiled at me. Gabriel returned about a half hour
later in a suit, his bangs were a mess. I looked up and
laughed.

"What's so funny?" He asked me.

"Daddy, your hair is all messy!" Ethan exclaimed.

"Oh," He said as he paused and ran his hand down the
front of his hair to straighten it.

"Good thing I have you around to let me know when I
don't look right!" Gabriel bent down and picked Ethan up
out of his chair, stood him on the floor and told him to get
his stuff together.

"Looking forward to this evening Kensie, I really don't
want to leave you now, I can think of 2000 things we could
do in LA today but I can't get out of this meeting." Gabriel
sighed.

"It's okay, do what you have to do. Thank you for
spending time with me yesterday, it was great." I said with a
smile.

"You going to tell me tonight what it is you were going to
tell me?" He said as he poked me in the side.

"Nope." I laughed.

"You'll tell me eventually, I know you will." He smiled as
he kissed my nose.

"You think so?" I laughed as we walked outside to his car.

"The suspense will kill me, I will hold you hostage in my
basement, force you to play slop pool, and never feed you."
He laughed back.

"Oh, your threats, they scare me so." I laughed as I got
into the car.

"You know you mean a lot to me, right?" Gabriel said as
he drove down the drive way.

"I'd like to think so." I said looking down when he
entered the password into the gate.

"You'd like to think so?" He said looking at me with a
blank look.

"It was a joke; I know how much you mean to me…" I said and stopped.

I was so close to taking that note out of my purse, but I didn't.

"I know this trip has been crazy, and I hope that you have been able to see some interesting things, and I know the timing is off…" He stopped.

"It's fine, really, I am thankful I got to take a vacation. You really don't have to apologize." I said as I cut him off. *Timing is always off for me*; I thought but didn't say it.

When they dropped me off at the hotel, Gabriel got out of the car and opened my door, he gave me a huge hug and kissed me. It was a pretty in depth kiss. I melted, again. I really needed to learn to control that. I wanted to tell him I loved him, and that I never stopped loving him, I started to drift off thinking maybe if I told him that, we would stand in the street and hug each other forever, and then he would cancel everything he had going on for the day and spend it with me, watching movies, making out, and THEN, I would lay on his chest and listen to his heart beat.

As he released me, I felt like everyone was watching again, but he hurried up and got back in the car. Ethan waved to me as they drove off. He was the sweetest little boy, I could keep him forever.

Chapter 9-Moving On

When I got back to my room, I took a shower, and sat on the bed trying to decide if I should go sight-seeing or lay pool side again.

I decided to go sight-seeing. After all, I wasn't going to be there too much longer, and I wasn't going to waste it away at the hotel.

I remembered seeing this little place called "Wonders of the World" when we were going through Santa Monica the first day I came so I decided I wanted to go there first. After finding the building, they opened at four and it was only 2:30 so I figured I would stop at the café and eat a salad; hoping that took up an hour and a half.

When I walked into the café, I immediately spotted Spencer with some girl; she was really, really pretty, immaculately beautiful. They were eating lunch; I was a bit embarrassed and hoped he didn't see me. I had no idea why I was a bit jealous of seeing him with someone else, that wasn't my place. I began to wonder if that's the only place he eats, or gets coffee for that matter. I wasn't here to see him anyway, but, I rushed out of the café as quick as I could; praying he didn't see me.

I stopped at another little restaurant a few blocks over and had some soup and a sandwich. I sat there reading my book but I had no idea what it was about. My mind was headed in a million and one directions. I didn't know what I was doing anymore. I knew in my heart that I had begun to fall for Spencer, it was almost like an unobtainable, destined, exciting fluke for me; like my destiny had a loop hole and I had found it. On the other hand, I really wanted to be with Gabriel, I wanted so badly for it to be everything I had come to know. I realized that our lives were much too different now to have what I fell in love with.

I decided to take a cab to the pier. I perched myself along the beach and realized I had hardly taken any pictures of anything since I had been there. I didn't bring my suit, but I took out some paper from my purse and began writing what I was feeling down in poetic form. I took out my camera and started taking pictures of people, the ocean, whatever.

I wanted to get pictures of Gabriel's club too. I had to show Nora, speaking of which, my mental note must not have stuck because I forgot to call her. Sometimes I am amazed at how random my thoughts are. I suddenly remembered I needed to call her because I wanted pictures to show her. I felt like a really bad friend. I called my mom to check on the girls, they were eating dinner so I talked to my mom for about ten minutes and the girls for five minutes. They really didn't have much to say to me. As a matter of fact, they both got into a fight as Marie was on the phone with me over Rayanne playing with something Marie just had. My mom took the phone from her and then yelled at them in the back ground. It was comical to me, since I wasn't there, and I was glad I wasn't there.

I could hear the frustration in my mom's voice, and it's amazing that until you are away from your children and hear someone else do the same thing you do on a regular basis, you really don't realize how bad it sounds...they are just kids. That changed a lot of how I felt about my girls, they were mine, two people who I unconditionally loved, two people who I would never fall in and out of love with, two people who loved me back, and although they made me very mad sometimes, I needed to learn to control my voice with them, because it isn't their fault I get frustrated because I'm miserable.

I called Nora, she didn't answer. I called work, just to say hi, I didn't really know why, but I was friends with some of the girls in the office and wanted to check on things.

They were tied up on another line so I realized it was another bad timing situation. I took a walk along the beach shore in the sun for a few hours and went back to get some water. It was about 6:30 and I realized that I should probably head back if I wanted to go to that "Wonders of The World" place.

I started taking random pictures of the beach again, and I look over, see this guy who looked like Spencer standing at the edge of the beach in shorts, no shirt, no hat, facing the ocean. He had his hands on his hips, his back towards me. I started looking around for the girl I had seen him eating with earlier. *Did he bring her here? Was it even him?* I took a picture because he looked like a model whoever he was. He was almost perfect, almost like he was in the deepest thought anyone could be in.

I decided I'd walk over and see if it was him, I'd casually say hi, no big deal. Just see how he reacted, this time it might look like I was stalking him. Once I got to where he was standing, he was gone. Just like that, took my eyes off him for five seconds, gone. I got back on the bus and headed to the "Wonders of the World" building.

I spent about two hours there looking at all the art work and rocks; they had all kinds of neat stuff. There were lots of couples in there holding hands, looking at everything. I started to think about how awesome it would be if Gabriel were with me, but he probably wouldn't be interested if he were with me.

After I left I headed back to the hotel. Gabriel still hadn't called. I watched a bit of television, but nothing good was on. I sat down on the bed; it was comfortable, but not as comfortable as being on Gabriel's couch the night before. I loved being held as I fell asleep, but I didn't technically wake up with him holding me. Somehow we drifted apart; just like in reality, over the years. I must have nodded off because before I knew it, there was a knock on my hotel door.

I looked at the clock when my eyes focused and it said 2:00. I couldn't believe I slept that long. I immediately looked for my phone but I couldn't find it. I looked out the peep hole and it was someone from the hotel. I opened it and it was the hotel manager.

"I was asked to come and check to see if you were in the room miss. We tried to ring your phone but you did not answer." He said nicely.

"I didn't hear it ring, I am fine. I must have fallen asleep. May I ask who "we" is?" I said confused.

"Gabriel Jack Miss. He was trying to reach you." He said with sincerity.

"I'm fine, thank you for checking on me, I appreciate it. I will call him." I said with a half awake smile.

"If there is anything we can do for you, let us know immediately." He offered.

"Thank you." I said again.

When I shut the door I said out loud, *"What the hell? Who does that?"* I started to search for my phone. It was in the bed. I had three missed calls; two from Gabriel, and one from an unknown number, but I thought I had seen it before.

I decided to call Gabriel back before I listened to my voice mails. I sat back down on the bed.

"Where the heck have you been?" Gabriel yelled without even saying hello.

"I fell asleep on my bed, must have rolled over on top of my cell and I didn't hear it, I just woke up." I said back apologizing.

"I was worried about you. I'm glad you are okay, I couldn't get over there to see if you were in your room and we tried to ring your hotel room phone, you didn't answer." Gabriel explained.

"I didn't hear it ring." I leaned over the bed to check the phone, the ringer was off.

"So, are you up to hanging out tonight, I know it's late and I understand if you're not." Gabriel asked.

"I'm going to stay here; I am really tired for some reason. You can come here, if you want..." I said kind of asking.

"I would love to but Ethan is in bed, his mother had to take her grandmother to the hospital and dropped him off on her way." Gabriel explained.

"I'm sorry to hear that, hope everything is okay, I think I will just sleep it off and let you spend time with Ethan." I answered.

"Okay, I hope you have a good night's rest Kensie, and by the way, I am going to the fourth street promenade, it isn't far from where you are to check out some local talent in the morning. I would like for you to come with me, if you want to." Gabriel said sweetly.

"I'd love to go." I said.

"I'll call you around noon, sweet dreams." Gabriel said.

I tried to fall back to sleep, I tried to watch television. I listened to my voice mails from the three calls I missed. The two from Gabriel were just telling me to call him so he knew where I was. The unknown number was from Spencer. He called in-between Gabriel's two calls at midnight. He just said to call him because he was worried about me. I sat for a minute and thought about it. I called Nora; once again, it was late, or early in Tennessee.

"Hello?" Nora answered in a confused and dazed voice.

"I know it's early, and I'm sorry, but I tried to call you a couple of times, haven't heard from you but I really need to talk to you." I said painfully.

"What's going on Kensie, are you okay?" Nora said half awake.

"Yes, I'm fine. I am torn, torn between knowing what's real and what's not and some hope of reconciliation and the thought of falling in love all over again." I said with tears in my eyes.

"What's going on? Has he changed that much, or is it great and you don't know how to deal with it?"

"It isn't him, I like him, I think, or thought. I loved him; I guess I didn't come here to fall in love again, I guess I just wanted to get away and see what it felt like after all these years. I know life doesn't work like this, I don't want to fall in love, maybe, I don't know what I want." I began to cry harder. "I have spent more time with his best friend than I have him and the time I have spent with him has been wonderful, but he's really busy. It seems like the timing is all off, just like every other relationship I have had. I can't stop thinking about his best friend." I finished almost unable to breathe.

"Does he know this? Does he feel the same?" Nora asked.

"I don't think so, I mean, no, of course he doesn't. He's a player, I mean, or at least I think he is. He is so cute and Nora, he makes me smile, I feel it. He's down to earth, drives a car I would never own, and I don't know why I like him so much; it doesn't make any sense." I said.

"Well, I think you just gave me several reasons why you like him, dear." Nora comforted.

"I know he would never like me like that, I have kids, he doesn't even want kids, I have nothing to offer him; I have nothing to offer either one of them really. They are successful, and they basically know where they are going." I added.

"Maybe you should talk to Gabriel, the point of going was to hang out with him, right?" Nora asked.

"I fell asleep earlier and they both called me, I called Gabriel back but it's too late to call Spencer back, but I feel like I should." I told her.

"I guess it is what it is, if he called you, call him back, then call me in the morning and let me know how things went. I have got to get back to sleep Kensie; I have to get up in two hours." Nora said in a tired voice.

"UGH! I hate that phrase. 'It is what it is' is the most ridiculous this anyone could say." I said sarcastically as I mocked her. "You know I love you to death but it isn't what it is, I want you to fix it so I can move on." I finally yelled.

"You know I can't do that Kensie. You have to fix this on your own." She said back calmly.

"I know, I'm sorry, you are right, I'll call you tomorrow." I said as I hung up the phone.

I thought about it for a few minutes. Although none of us had really texted each other, I chickened out of calling him and I texted him. It just said: "I got your voicemail a bit ago when Gabriel had the hotel manager check on me-I fell asleep on my phone and I know it's late but I wanted you to know I am okay." Then I hit send. My heart was pounding. *What if he was with that girl? What if he was with Gabriel?* Oh well, it was done. I put my phone in my lap and stared at it for what felt like forever but more like ten minutes.

Nothing; I tried to watch some television, but there was nothing on. I realized that although I analyzed the similarities between Spencer and Gabriel, Spencer was the first guy I didn't compare to Gabriel. Gabriel couldn't be compared to Gabriel because we weren't kids any more.

Spencer was a separate person, one I really didn't compare to Gabriel at all. That was ground breaking. It was like a huge weight was lifted. I realized that I didn't have to keep comparing guys to Gabriel, because it really wasn't about him, it was about being in love. It wasn't about him; it was about truly loving some body as much as they love you. That was what true love meant to me.

About fifteen minutes later, my phone vibrated and sang with a new text message flashing on it. I anxiously opened it and it said:

"Hey, was just sitting here watching TV, glad u texted, I was worried about u."

I texted back-shaking: "I was tired. You weren't by any chance @ the pier today were you?"

A few minutes later he texted back: "I was, were you there?"

I struggled to find words to write. I started to write "I also seen you at the café with some girl" but I erased it. It wasn't my business, so I wrote: "I thought I seen you but I went to say hi and you were gone."

He texted back immediately: "I didn't see you."

I hate texting. You never know what the person is meaning or if they are hateful or being silly, or any emotion for that matter. I texted back: "Well, I'll let you go, it's late."

He didn't text back. I was immediately sorry I said that, but I didn't really want to stop talking to him. I really didn't want to say that.

A half hour later he texted back: "It isn't that late." I smiled as I wrote: "Are you drunk?" He replied with: "Nope, not at all, not a drink all day." I smiled again.

I was hoping he wasn't sitting there with that girl and I was interrupting. I ran out of things to say so I laid there in the dark.

"You still awake?" He texted back.

"I am. Watching nothing on TV." I replied.

"Me too. You want me to call you?" He wrote.

"If you want…I would like that." I wrote back.

He called me about fifteen minutes later and I was bit uneasy at first. I didn't know what to say.

"How come you didn't just call me?" He asked.

"I didn't know what you were doing and it was 2:30 but I hoped you got text messages." I said.

"I was doing nothing, I couldn't sleep, have a lot on my mind." He said.

"Do you want to talk about it?" I said because I wanted to comfort him.

"Not really, just thinking of going home for a while, I need a break." He said as he paused.

"I can totally understand that, it seems hectic around here." I gave him my best mom voice.

"I haven't seen my parents in a while, I miss them, and as stupid as it sounds, my dog." He said sadly.

"I think tomorrow we are going to the fourth street promenade to see some performing artists. Are you coming?" I asked him.

"I'm not sure yet." He said. "How was your day?" He added after a silent pause.

"Pretty good actually, I did some sight-seeing, which was really cool." I said in my most tired voice.

"So, if I pulled up outside the hotel, can you run out for a second?" Spencer asked.

"Sure, you okay?" I said unsettled.

"Yeah, I just have something I need to give you; I forgot to give it to you the other day." He replied.

"Okay, when?" I asked.

"I'll be there in about twenty minutes." He said.

"I'll be looking for you." I replied as I said goodbye and closed my cell phone.

I waited by the door, the bell boy just kept staring at me. I just said under my breath, '*meeting a friend*' and watched for Spencer's car. He probably thought I was a drug addict it was so late, or early I guess you could say.

He pulled up in front of the building and I went outside. I had on a pair of shorts, tee shirt, no bra, geez I bet I looked hot. It was all good because when he opened the car door for me to get in; he had on a long pair of basketball shorts, a tee shirt, and some flip flops. We pulled up to the nearest parking spot and stopped. He reached between his seats and pulled out this box; wrapped in red paper.

"I can't believe you are up so late." I said trying to break my nervousness.

"Like I said, it isn't that late, I've been up later." He laughed.

Spencer handed me the box, I opened it slowly. It was a necklace and gold earrings that matched the bracelet my dad got me when I was sixteen. I never took it off. *How much money did we make that night bartending?* I know he said it was a fair amount, but it looked expensive.

"It's beautiful!" I said as I tried to take it out of the box. "It matches my bracelet, I love it!" I exclaimed.

Spencer took out the necklace and put it around my neck. I don't think anyone besides my dad ever bought me anything that pretty, except for my mom who, on occasion, bought me a nice set of earrings.

"I hope you like it." He said as he clasped it around my neck.

"I love it, how much did it cost? How much DID we make that night?" I said.

"Not as much as your worth, it wasn't a lot anyway. I just wanted you to have it. I saw it and thought of your bracelet." Spencer smiled.

"I don't know what to say, I love it." I smiled back.

He was actually paying some bit of attention to me, he had to have been, or maybe not, the bracelet I had wasn't hard to miss, it wasn't gaudy, just a standard rope chain bracelet with diamond dust in it, just then it occurred to me that it all matched my ring my grandma gave me. I almost cried.

"I'm glad you like it." Spencer said with a huge smile.

Although he looked like he rolled out of bed, like I had actually awakened him up with my text message, he was still beautiful. I wanted to ask him if he had been asleep and apologize for waking him up.

I gave Spencer a hug and didn't really know what to say. "I guess I better get back up to my room, gotta attempt to get some sleep."

"Goodnight Kensie, next time call me, I will answer."

"Thank you." I smiled as I got out of the car.

I walked back up the block to the hotel wondering how he could be so sweet. *What is really wrong with him?* I thought to myself. He drove all the way over here and I just let him leave. *What should I have done?* I decided to call him back.

"Kensie?" Spencer said as he answered his phone, "Is everything okay?" He finished.

"I guess I didn't really want you to leave, but I need to sleep and now I'm not tired, and I want you to know I appreciate the necklace more than you will ever know." I said before he could even say another word.

"I was going to see if you wanted to get some early breakfast but you didn't have any shoes on." He laughed.

"Yeah, I guess I would have needed those. You should have said something and I would have dressed better." I laughed back.

We talked a little bit about his family, he had some music on but I couldn't make it out.

"I just really want to see them for a while." Spencer added as I heard him opening his door awhile later and I heard him turn on the light. Mostly it was silent between us but we both started laughing about the silence at the same time.

"That's the quietest I have ever heard on the end of the phone. I almost asked if you were still there." Spencer said laughing again.

"I am here, I could hear you breathing…and walking up the steps and turning the light on. So, I saw you today, not just at the pier." I couldn't take it anymore; it was in the back of my mind the whole time.

"Where at?" Spencer asked inquisitively.

"The café." I answered.

"Why didn't you say hi?" He asked.

"You were with a girl and I know how girls are, they get upset if their time is interrupted by someone else." I laughed but meant it.

"Oh yeah, I had lunch with Amanda. She's an old friend; we worked on our first screen play together. She was asking me for advice on a new project she is working on. She actually works for Gabriel at the club; she helps out with the bar when he needs her. It's too bad she couldn't help out the other night, but we did fine." He added.

"I didn't know so I didn't say anything." I said.

"You should have said hi, she isn't my girl or anything." I could hear him drinking something and he continued, "I told you, I am not relationship material. I don't keep a girlfriend, it isn't anything personal, but, it's not like I am out trying to spot the next girl for the evening. I just tell them right off, I am not trying to be in a relationship at the moment." He finished.

"I guess that's kind of how I feel. I want to wait until my girls are older, that way there is less stress straight from the beginning." I said agreeing with him.

"I can understand that." Spencer said.

After a few minutes of silence, it seemed like we ran out of things to say.

"Well, I guess it's getting really late, or early, so I will let you go and try to get some sleep Spencer." I said.

"Goodnight Kensie, thanks for calling me, I mean texting me earlier." He laughed.

"Thank you, for the gift, it's beautiful." I said back.

After we got off the phone, I just sat there twisting the necklace around and around. I sat in silence. Finally, at 6:30 in the morning, I fell asleep. I think my cell phone rang like thirty times from 8:30 to 10:30. I was too tired to remember. My mom called, the girls wanted to say hi, guess I did tell her I was going to call this morning. Spencer called, Gabriel called twice, and Nora called. The other day no one really wanted to talk to me.

I called my mom back first and talked to my girls. They started to seem like they missed me but didn't talk to me long. My mom seemed like something was bothering her but she didn't say what it was. I figured Rayanne was driving her nuts. I called Spencer, he didn't answer.

I called Gabriel back, I kind of felt guilty for talking to Spencer last night but whatever, kind of weird that he was the reason I was letting go of Gabriel, somewhat, but at the same time, if Ethan hadn't been dropped off, I'd never have had that conversation with Spencer, and everything happens for a reason, Ironic.

"HI KENSIE!" Gabriel exclaimed when he answered.

"You are cheery this morning." I said still half awake.

"You ready to go see some of the best street performances of your life?" He asked.

"That all depends on when it is; I need coffee." I laughed as I got out of bed. I really had to pee but I didn't want to do it while I was on the phone with him.

"Walk down the end of your street, make a right and follow that street up to fourth, in an hour or so, you'll see me, Ethan, and Spencer some where there. But don't look too hard for us because I want you to give me your opinion on these performances." He noted.

"Okay, I'm getting ready now." I said as I walked into the bathroom. Ugh, I looked like hell. My mascara made the under part of my eyes black, I hoped they didn't look like that last night. I never even looked at myself before going outside to meet Spencer.

"See you there!" Gabriel said before I could even realize I was still on the phone with him.

I got in the shower and looked at myself in the mirror. *Do I hide my necklace? Do I wear it with pride?* Oh well, it's just a necklace, and besides, I made the money, it isn't like he just gave it to me as a gift. So I braided my hair back, put on my shorts and my tank top. I still had a couple of outfits that I brought with me, but nothing looked appealing. I walked the way Gabriel told me to and got a text from Spencer.

"Where are you?" He messaged.

"I'm on my way." I texted back.

"We are walking around, wanted to make sure you were up =)" He sent back with a smiley face.

That kind of made me happy. I bet I walked around looking for them for an hour but it was really cool. The performers were really good. I stopped to watch some of them, holding my coffee I bought from a vendor. I felt a light tug on my leg. I looked down and it was Ethan.

"Hello Ethan! Are you having fun?" I said.

"Yes, it is cool; I have never seen these peoples before." He smiled.

Peoples. It made me laugh because it reminded me so much of Marie. Gabriel came walking up to me a few minutes later holding an ice cream. He looked ridiculous; he had on a gangster hat, grunge pants, a tan shirt, and brown shoes.

"We stopped for ice cream. There are some good acts out here. I am trying to get information from them so I can give it to the casting agents. In the screen play they go to a fair and there are street performers so they will blend in perfect." Gabriel offered.

"Nice outfit." I said as I looked him up and down.

"Incognito. Not that they won't know who I am as soon as I start getting names but, I'm not worried about it." He said as he started watching the guy next to us break dancing.

"You should write me in, I'm just kidding. But those guys over there are really gooooo." I said as I pointed to the guys next to us.

Spencer walked up with that girl he had lunch with yesterday. He smeared chocolate ice cream on my cheek and licked it off before I uttered the "d" out of my mouth to finish the word good.

"Oh, you got games, huh?" I took his container of ice cream.

"Don't do it, this is a new shirt...don't do it!" Spencer exclaimed as he hid behind Gabriel.

"Okay, okay." I said as I handed it back to him.

"This is Amanda, Kensie; she is a friend of ours." Spencer introduced her to me.

I shook her hand and she politely said hello.

"Nice necklace, is it new?" Gabriel asked me as he looked at my neck intently.

"It is; the good people of Santa Monica who loved their beer bought it for me." I concluded.

"Very pretty." Gabriel said as he gave Spencer a glare.

Spencer shrugged his shoulders and picked Ethan up to hold him above the crowd. Gabriel started taking down names of some performers and starting talking to people.

"You really made a mess out of their lives." Amanda laughed as we walked past the three of them.

"I'm sorry?" I said confused.

"Oh, I had lunch with Spencer yesterday and apparently they are both trying to get your attention." Amanda said as we walked way ahead of them.

"What do you mean?" I said as I scrunched my forehead.

"Spencer said Gabriel ripped his ass open for hanging out with you at the Casino and asked him if he slept with you, which really pissed Spencer off." She started to inform me. "I guess Spencer told him you have a good heart and you are looking for more than he can give you." She finished.

"How would he know?" I asked her.

"He said Gabriel asked him not to hang out with you the rest of the time you were here and he basically told him to screw off." She laughed.

"What the? What is his problem?" I asked her.

"You like Spencer don't you?" She asked me.

"I like him, I like both of them. I just don't want to get my feelings hurt. I'm not going to be here much longer." I replied. This girl liked to talk. I barely know her and she's giving me the low-down. I started to analyze her intentions. *Was she mad at me, was she just trying to help?* She knew both of them better than I did.

"I guess Gabriel told him that he wanted to be more to you, but he can't. I'm just throwing that out there because Spencer briefly let me in on your past with Gabriel, I wasn't trying to pry and I hope you don't mind." She said.

"Mind that Spencer is talking about me, not at all!" I laughed.

"It's just, I know these guys, I know you have known Gabriel a lot longer but you don't really know the more recent version." She chuckled.

"I don't know, Spencer really hasn't said or done anything wrong. He hasn't tried to get with me or anything of the sort and I didn't sleep with Gabriel when we were together. I have actually had a great time and that's all I intended to do while I was here." I told her.

"I haven't seen Spencer in any relationship that he fought for, or that lasted longer than two months, but he never stopped talking about you, which was strange for him and I've known him for a while." She finished.

Gabriel and Spencer were now right behind us and we both seen them in a window reflection. We stopped talking about the conversation and continued to walk forward. I could see Spencer make a hand notation in the reflection of '650'. *Are you serious?* I know we didn't make that much money that night. I didn't act like I even seen it. I just grabbed Ethan's hand and directed him towards some more street performers. We were there for about an hour and Spencer ending up leaving with Amanda. He waved as he left. I was concerned as to why he didn't say anything.

"Where did Spencer go?" I asked Gabriel.

"He went home, why?" Gabriel asked me.

"Just thought it was weird he didn't say bye." I said.

"You like him don't you?" Gabriel asked me.

"Jealous much?" I asked him back.

"Just asking." Gabriel said as he directed Ethan around the corner.

I didn't know what to say; I wanted to say yeah, I like both of you and wish I could roll the two of you up in one person. I didn't.

"So I was wondering if you wanted to go to the pier later. I am taking Ethan home in about an hour and thought I would pick you up after that, if you want to." Gabriel finally said.

"Sure, that sounds great to me; I'd love to see it at night." I said back smiling.

"Do you want a ride back to the hotel?" Gabriel asked taking Ethan from me.

"No, thank you though, I don't mind walking." I said back.

We gave each other a hug and I started to turn back down the street to head to the hotel while looking for my phone in my purse. I called Spencer as soon as I was out of Gabriel's eye sight.

"Hey, why did you leave earlier without saying bye?" I said when Spencer answered.

"I don't know, I guess I think I am getting too close to you and Gabriel doesn't like it much." He replied.

"He is the one who introduced you to me and had you play baby sitter when he couldn't." I said hastily.

"I already told you it wasn't like that Kensie." Spencer said in a frustrated voice.

"Then explain to me why you can't say bye to me? That makes no sense." I said.

"I guess it became uncomfortable. He told me I should have just given you the money we made instead of getting you that necklace, I didn't think it was that big of a deal, it's not like I asked you to marry me or anything." Spencer said laughing.

"Well, I loved it and I don't care if he gets mad or not. I like you, you're fun to be around and I'd appreciate it if you didn't walk away like that, without even saying bye." I said with a scratch in my voice. "I'd like to think we are friends and I hope we can remain friends after I'm gone." I finished.

"For sure." Spencer said.

"I'll let you go, I just wanted to ask you what was up." I replied.

"I'll talk to you later." Spencer said and hung up.

I wanted to call Gabriel and ask him what the problem was, but I didn't want him to know I called Spencer, and I didn't want to come between them. I didn't really know why, we hadn't done anything. There was no reason to get mad, sure, I thought he was hot, and he was sweet, but after fifteen years of waiting, I came there to be with Gabriel, or so I wanted to believe.

After I got back to the hotel, I went back to the pool to finish reading some more of my book. There weren't a lot of people there so it was nice and quiet. I actually got half way through it when I decided to go back to my room and relax a bit. Gabriel still hadn't called, that was one long hour. I was running out of things to think of, if someone had given me a map, I'd probably been half way across Santa Monica by now finding things to do. At least it seemed like I could have been.

I realized I had only spent about $400 so this trip really hadn't been that bad. The guys had been paying for everything I ate so that was pretty cool. *I should be finding a nice restaurant and actually sitting down to eat some real food,* I thought to myself. I ended up walking down to the main lobby and asking for anything they might have on Santa Monica. The lady at the front desk gave me a nice brochure. Just as I sat down to read through it, Gabriel called. I went back to my room and put on a pair of shorts and a tee shirt, I didn't really attempt to get dressed up to go to the pier. No makeup, didn't do my hair, who cares anyway.

Gabriel picked me up from the hotel some time later and we drove to the pier.

"I got you something." He said as we pulled into the pier.

"Awe, what is it?" I said.

Gabriel reached behind his seat and pulled out a bag, I opened it and it was two hats. They both were very nice, one was a White Sox hat; one was a Yankees hat. I smiled. That meant a lot to me. It may not have been as expensive as Spencer's gift, but it was the concept that counted.

"I told you I'd get you a good hat to wear." Gabriel laughed.

"I love them!" I smiled.

"Not as expensive as Spencer's gift, but…" He said as I cut him off.

"That wasn't really a gift, I worked for that money and this means just as much to me as this necklace." I said.

"That's good because I got you something else." He said as he reached behind his seat.

He pulled out a picture frame, it was in a nice wooden frame, it was an 8x10 of him and I when we were about eight on a swing set at the park. I was in the swing, he was pushing me. The picture was a close-up; I had never seen it before. My braids and brown eyes were bright in the sun, as was his blond hair and blue eyes. That picture was just how I remembered our childhood to be. That was one memory that I had forgotten about. I immediately began to get teary eyed.

"I can't believe you have a picture, I have never seen this before. Who took it?" I said as I looked up at Gabriel.

"My mom took it. I keep it on my night stand in my bedroom, it has always been there. If anyone ever asked me who it was, I always told them, my best friend." Gabriel said as he wiped the tear away and then got out of the car.

He opened my door and helped me out of the car. We walked up to the beach and stopped. It was quiet along the beach but the pier itself was busy and bright. It was really beautiful.

"It's nice here, at night. I haven't been down here in a while. I don't get out much between the club and work." Gabriel said. "You know, things haven't gone exactly as I planned them to but I'm really glad you came." Gabriel finished.

"I'm glad I'm here too, I have been able to see a lot of things, and I really am thankful you invited me." I told him.

We ended up sitting on the beach. He was behind me. I sat in front of him; he put his arms around my waist and his chin on my shoulder. *Why was I starting to think this was a game? A game between the two of them, to see which one ended up sleeping with me?* I was bound set and determined that was not going to happen. I would chance going back to Tennessee feeling the "what might have been", or the "what could have happened" instead of the guilt I might feel later. That just wasn't me.

Oh well, I thought, I wasn't married anymore, I didn't belong to any body, I was going to play it by ear.

"It's so pretty right now." Gabriel said as the sun began to set.

"SHIT! MY CAMERA!" I yelled. "I should be taking pictures of this, I promised the girls lots of pictures and I have hardly taken any of anything I have done." I whined.

"I'll take some on my phone and send them to you, they will turn out great, I promise, go stand over there..." Gabriel said as he pointed.

I stood up and walked over to where he pointed, there was a rock that I sat on and he took a couple of pictures. Then I walked back over to him and he put his camera out in front of us and snapped a couple of us together. I took a stick nearby and drew a heart shape in the sand. He took a picture of that too. He sent them to my phone and it made me feel good that he used his phone to take them. We sat for a while and talked about our goals and where we wanted to be in a few years. There was some much needed silence between us that lasted a bit longer than I wanted it to. Finally, I broke the silence.

"What do you think about love?" Gabriel asked me.

"I don't know, I guess I think that true love never dies. It's the kind that makes you melt, every time that person touches you, its affection and laughter. It's a smile that never goes away." I said as I watched the sky.

"I don't think I've ever felt that way." Gabriel said. I did not want to hear those words. Maybe he never felt for me like I did him. Maybe I wasted this entire time wanting something that didn't exist.

"I felt that way once, it never went away. I guess I am fortunate to have felt that way, some people live their whole lives never knowing what that feels like." I said.

"I hope that someday, you get that back Kensie, you are a wonderful, wonderful person and you have grown into a really special person. I am very sorry we ever lost track of each other." Gabriel said as he kissed my shoulder.

We sat there for a while in silence. I still didn't know what to say. I suddenly didn't want him to touch me, I became angry. I wanted to run to Spencer and cry, maybe he would make it better. There was so much I wanted to say but I couldn't count the times I wrote myself notes, and re-wrote them, how many times I was in relationships where I rattled off the first thing that came to my mind. For once, I was quiet.

"Well, I guess we should head back, I have to get to the club tonight." Gabriel said.

"I think I'm going to stay in tonight, I don't feel much like going to the club." I replied.

"You aren't going to come out tonight?" He said in a hurt voice.

"I've done more walking in the last few days than I have in the last few months." I said as I laughed.

"Okay, I'll take you back to the hotel, you promise to call me in the morning?" Gabriel said as he scooted around to face me.

"Yes, I promise." I said looking him directly into his blue eyes. The eyes I couldn't stop thinking about for the last fifteen years, the eyes that used to let me see through to his soul.

The drive back to the hotel was pretty silent. He kept looking over at me and I just stared straight ahead. When we got back to the hotel, Gabriel walked me to my room, came in the room and sat on my bed.

"Promise me you will call in the morning?" He asked honestly.

"I will, I said I would, I have never lied to you, I won't start now, silly; I really am tired." I said as I started fluffing my pillows.

Gabriel looked in the bathroom. *What was he looking for?* Maybe he was used to doing inspections of places he usually wasn't in without some of his entourage. I didn't know, didn't ask. I sat down on the bed and he walked over and held his hands out to me. I put my hands out and he grabbed mine, pulling me up close to him.

He kissed me and gave me a huge hug, but he didn't let go right away. I didn't want him to let go; but he did. My emotions were so over the edge that I had no idea what I wanted. After he left, I thought about how I wished he would have stayed, but I knew it was for the best. When he kissed me, I really didn't feel butterflies anymore; I think that hurt the most.

I had a great trip so far, it was a bit confusing but it was great to get away. *So what do you do when you can't decide what you are doing?* I sat on the bed for a while, I didn't know what I was going to say to him; to know he never loved me like I loved him was a hard thing to bear. I could never tell him how I felt now, not the truth, the ironic thing is, maybe-I no longer wanted to.

I got out my lap top to check my email. I had some emails from work, nothing major. I got on that social website, the one that I found Gabriel on, and started playing some games. I had seen that Gabriel had been tagged in Spencer's page in a few pictures. I didn't know Spencer had one too. I looked at Spencer's page, it wasn't set to private. He had put the picture taken of us at the casino on there and underneath it was a picture of the ocean.

The sky mainly, but I had to look twice because the picture was titled "Beautiful" and there were all kinds of comments under it asking who was in the picture and when it was taken. He hadn't commented back yet, and that one wasn't tagged to Gabriel, but it was me, I swear, I know my back side. It was a very pretty picture, the sky was an off blue, the clouds looked like fluffy pillows, the water was coming in; there was a ripple underneath my feet. I was just standing there, my hair blowing in the wind, you could see the side of my face but that was it. I know it was me. *How in the world did he take that without my noticing? Why did he take it?* I shut off my lap top and sat there for a few seconds. I wanted to stalk his page but I decided not to.

So what if it was dark out, Spencer told me not to walk at night, *what did he know?* I can handle my own. It wasn't like Santa Monica was LA or something. I walked down to this pharmacy, I needed some cold cream for my face; it was beginning to peal. I walked past an isle that had candles on it; I wondered if I would be able to take that on the plane. I bought one anyway. I just knew when I got back to the hotel; I was going to burn it; even if we weren't supposed to.

I walked back to my room, feeling really depressed. I sat on my bed and watched some television show that was probably funny in a parallel universe, but not in the one I was in right now.

I lit the candle, I couldn't help it-it was lilac and smelled so good. I took the note I had wrote, the one that was in my purse for forever in a day, and held it up to the candle. It caught fire immediately. I dropped it into the candle and watched it burn right to the end. I wasn't ready to part with it yet, so I blew out the candle and when it cooled down, I gathered up the ashes and stuck them in a baggie. I thought about those words over and over until I finally fell asleep.

He used to call me Ken, I wore overalls and climbed trees.
When we were four, he thought I was a boy.
He started calling me K as we grew older, he brought me
flowers he picked in the fields.
I missed him when I didn't see him,
It took all my strength not to tell him how I felt,
I loved my best friend, I could never say goodbye,
I missed his smile, I missed his voice.
If he had known would it have ended, would he have kept in
touch; how did he not know he had my heart?
I won't let myself forget him, I won't lose faith that I will
see him again, and then, I will tell him…I love him.

Chapter 10-Analysis

The next morning when I woke up, I called Gabriel but he didn't answer. I didn't leave a message. Maybe it was too early for him. I didn't know what to do for the day so I decided to go to the hotel bar and get a drink.

Maybe a drink would get it all off my mind; all of it. About an hour into my morning drink, Gabriel called me and told me he, once again, would be tied up for the day but I was more than welcome to come to the club later. I sat there talking to the hot bartender, all these guys around me who were smoking hot, I hadn't paid any attention to them, and I decided not to pick at this one. He was from Ohio, spiked brown hair, he wasn't very tall but I started telling him my story for some reason. He told me I needed to leave both guys alone and move on about my business. I laughed.

He was actually intelligent, seemed like a nice guy, BUT, he was recently married and just had a baby girl. I told him how girls could be a handful and shared some of my stories. Another hour had passed and I paid my tab. I decided to take a cab to Gabriel's house because I had enough of the day time 'I'm busy' situation.

As we drove by the house, the cab driver asked me if I wanted to pull up to the gate, I told him no, I would get out and walk up to the drive. I told the cab driver to wait for me until I told him it was okay to go, just in case he wasn't home. I didn't know if I would even be able to get in, but I was going to try it. As I walked up the drive to the gate, I saw Gabriel getting into a car with some girl, and Spencer leaving in his car, with some girl. I couldn't really tell who the girls were, but I knew it was Spencer and Gabriel.

What's going on? I was so disgusted that I ran down the drive way and jumped back into the cab and told him to take me back to the hotel. I was furious. *Did they just wake up?* I have never been so mad in my life. Right then, right there, I decided that I would make this my last evening and play their game.

Spencer called me when I got back to the hotel, I ignored it. He left me a message telling me he was going to go wash his car and go for a motorcycle ride if I wanted to join him. *Yeah, right,* I thought to myself. *Why would I call him when he was just with some girl, at Gabriel's?* I left my cell phone lying on the bed and went back down to the hotel bar, got a couple more drinks and went to the pool with my book that I really had no interest in. I had no idea what I read because I just kept thinking about how much Gabriel had changed, and how he really wasn't the person I thought he was. I decided this time I was going to swim, it might not have been the ocean, but it was a pool, *with water*, which meant I should be swimming.

I realized when I heard the lady next to me tell her son that it was three that I really should have my phone on me just in case something happened with the girls, so I went back up stairs and got my phone. Gabriel had called me around two; *did the two of them see me running away from Gabriel's house?* I didn't call him back. I called Nora. I explained to her what had happened.

"What are you going to do?" Nora asked me.

"Drink more." I said as I finished my margarita I brought upstairs with me.

"Don't get yourself in to trouble, Kensie. You aren't at home you know." She scolded.

"Oh, I'm not walking anywhere, I'm good." I reassured her.

Well, I love you, and I will see you when you get back, are you coming home tomorrow?" She asked.

"I hope so, I am going to have Gabriel call and change my flight since he paid for the ticket; otherwise I can't do anything about it until Saturday night." I said while looking through my purse to count what money I had left.

"Call me if you need me for anything." Nora said.

I went back to the bar and had another drink. This really hot guy sat beside me, he was magnificent, until he opened his mouth. He is one of those guys who are great eye candy but someone you cannot physically have a conversation with. I paid for my drink and went back upstairs.

I composed a song while I was sitting in my hotel room. I tried to hum the words to myself, and then I scratched it out, restarted it and ended with a poem/song. I was still trying to put music to the words I had written. Music was life to me, I don't know what I would ever do if I could not hear.

I decided I was going to get out the only thing I had left clean in my bag,-that damn dress Nora made me buy; and go to that club and dance my life away. I was half buzzed anyway. I had every intention of telling Gabriel what I thought about his inviting me to come see him and everything I felt.

I washed my hair, brushed it out, put on that sheer flowered dress. It came down pretty low in the front, but I kind of liked it once I got it on. I put on my open toed shoes and walked out of my hotel room. If I had any amount of substantial money left, I would have spent it all on clothes. The bell boy was staring at me, smiled really big as he held the door open, but I didn't really think I looked that great. I got a cab and went to the club.

When I got there, I didn't see anyone I knew so I went up to the first bar and ordered a margarita. There were some girls sitting next to me and we started chatting. I saw

Amanda at the other end of the bar, I waved and she came over and sat next to me.

"How are things going?" She asked me.

"Shitty." I replied.

"What's wrong?" She asked.

"I'm just ready to go home." I told her. "BUT, not before I hit that dance floor." I said as I downed my drink.

"I've been waiting to dance so let's go." She said as she pulled me off my bar stool. I kind of liked her; she seemed a lot like-me.

We walked out to the dance floor and a few hours later, I felt like I lost twenty pounds while I was dancing. She was beautiful, and she could dance, that girl could dance better than Nora and Nora had the hips and ass to shake, of course, she is the one who taught me how to do it right. I looked over and Spencer was standing offside on his phone. He waved. I ignored him. Amanda waved at him and we continued to dance. He looked over at us with a confused look on his face as he put his phone back in his pocket and I just kept dancing.

I checked my phone, he didn't call me, zero missed calls, I was happy that he might actually leave me alone. I went to the opposite bar and ordered another drink. Spencer walked towards me and I turned the opposite way and hurried back to the dance floor. I looked over and Gabriel was in the corner talking to some girl who had the same kind of clothes on the one he was with earlier had on.

That's fine, I thought to myself, *he'll talk to me eventually and I'll let him know I want to go home.* I turned around and Spencer was standing next to me in the middle of the dance floor.

"I called you earlier, why didn't you call me back and why are you avoiding me?" He said as he grabbed my arm.

"You don't dance, leave me alone and get off the dance floor, you're embarrassing me." I said jerking away from him but I never stopped dancing.

Amanda and I kept dancing and she had a strange look on her face, one that said, 'don't do it Kensie, you have no idea what you are in for.' I danced around Spencer to make him look stupid, just standing there like he expected some kind of explanation from me.

"What is wrong with you? Are you drunk?" Spencer asked as he grabbed my hands firmly.

"What is this? Some kind of game? I am going home tomorrow if I have to pay for it myself." I told him as I stopped dancing and we stood there in the middle of the dance floor looking like idiots.

Amanda patted Spencer on the back and walked off the dance floor to the bar. I stood there knowing I was not going to get away from talking to him.

"What the hell are you talking about?" Spencer said with an angry look on his face as he raised his voice high above the music.

"I went to Gabriel's house today, I seen the two of you with that girl over there, the one he is standing with right now, and you with some other girl. I guess the joke is on me." I yelled back.

"Wow, do you have that all wrong." He said and laughed. He tried to hug me but I didn't let it happen. He was laughing at me because I figured out their game and it made me even madder.

One of the girls I was talking to at the bar was dancing behind me and I could tell she was listening into mine and Spencer's conversation.

"You know Gabriel?" She asked me as she stopped dancing.

"Yeah, he's an old friend of mine, I used to think I loved him" I yelled as I walked off the dance floor. Spencer had a blank look on his face.

"How long have you known each other?" She asked as she followed me.

"I don't know, about 26 years or so, for as long as I can remember." I said.

"You need to leave." Spencer turned toward her and said.

"Are you guys together because I was just at his house last night." She smiled. "You're the girl in the picture." She laughed again.

I stopped right where I was, I had enough. 'The girl in the picture', wow, that was the only thing Gabriel didn't lie about. Spencer had followed us back to the bar and gently grabbed my arm again; in which I jerked away from him. This time he grabbed my hand and held it tight.

"You need to leave." He said to her again as he led me to the VIP room.

"It's not like that huh? Him giving you shit about being around me, this being some kind of joke, just last night he was with me at the pier, then he has this girl back at his house after he calls me and finds out I'm going to stay at the hotel... what the hell man? LET GO OF MY HAND" I yelled at Spencer.

"I'm going to let go of you, but I want you to listen to me...you really have this all wrong. Gabriel had a party at his house last night, it wasn't planned. That girl out there running her mouth used to date him; she showed up at his house and made a scene. Liam and Josh made her leave. The girl he is talking to is the director of the movie he's making and the girl I was with this morning was Ethan's mom. I played basketball all morning and Gabriel called me and asked me to pick her up from his house; they had been in a meeting with an attorney to sign some papers about Ethan because Gabriel is going to be out of the country in a few weeks." Spencer said without even catching a breath. Once he caught his breath, he continued, "She took a cab to his house because her grandmother is in the hospital and Gabriel couldn't go pick her up. Geez Kensie, why don't you ask somebody before you get mad?" Spencer finished as he rubbed his forehead with his fingers.

I stood there, half-drunk by now, wanting to get back to the dance floor, half not caring about what he was saying and half wondering if it were true. I was still mad, it all happened so fast and it seemed like I was stuck in the middle of my own stupidity. *What was I supposed to think?*

"I know you have been drinking, and I'm sorry that you didn't know what was going on, and I don't know what Gabriel's deal is about us hanging out, but I am not lying to you." Spencer said.

The girl I exchanged words with came into the VIP room yelling. She got in my face and started screaming at me. I was drunk, I didn't care, and really...*who was she anyway?* I didn't normally get involved in confrontation, but I didn't let anyone talk to me like that.

"I'm going to tell you one time, just once, to get out of my face." I said to her sternly.

Spencer got in between us and told her to leave, AGAIN. She continued to yell around him but she wasn't getting around him. She tried, he remained calm and he opened his phone to call some body. She knocked his phone out of his hands and it landed on the floor. I'm pretty sure that her touching his phone caused me to explode. As I watched his phone bounce off the ground, he bent over to pick it up. I leaned forward, and I blasted her.

He got in between us again and the security guards came in and grabbed both of us. By this time, there were people getting out their camera's, taking pictures and Gabriel came into the VIP room and told the security guard who was holding me to let go and escort her out.

How embarrassing! I was so mad, I just wanted to leave. Gabriel started apologizing to me.

"I came here to have fun, that bitch is crazy and if she comes at me again, I'm going to smash her face in the ground." I told Gabriel as mad as I could be.

"I'm sorry Kensie, I didn't even know she was here or she would have been gone a long time ago. I wasn't paying attention. I am very, very sorry." He said again.

"I'm sorry, I didn't mean to start a fight in your club, but she got in my face, she knocked Spencer's phone out of his hand, and I..." I apologized and stopped. "If you will excuse me, I came here to dance and that is what I am going to do." I finished saying as I walked away from Gabriel still pissed.

I felt bad; it really wasn't Gabriel's fault. I felt awful for Spencer, I went off on him when I really wanted to go off on Gabriel; he just happened to get caught in the middle of it. I didn't want to argue with either one of them. Spencer stood off side staring at me for a short period of time, then I saw Gabriel walk over to Spencer and they ended up going up to the office; they looked like they were arguing along the way.

I could see them from the dance floor, but I kept dancing. Another hour or so went by, it was now around three in the morning and I decided to head up to the office and tell Gabriel I wanted to go home. I was sobering up now, and it seemed like I caused enough issues for one night. Spencer walked out of the door, slammed it shut, and walked right past me.

"I'm going home tomorrow." I said as I stopped and turned around.

"Me too." He uttered as he stopped but never turned around.

"I'm sorry I yelled at you, it wasn't your fault." I said waiting for him to look at me.

"Same old story, I argue with everyone I ..." He paused and kept walking.

"Sixteen Candles." I yelled down the stairs.

"What?" He stopped again and said nastily.

"Sixteen Candles. That's my favorite movie." I stopped but didn't turn around. "I saw that movie on my sixteenth birthday and Sam reminded me of me, a normal girl who wanted the boy who didn't notice her. It's what kept me knowing anything is possible, sometimes people end up with people they never knew they could be with." I didn't look back; after a few minutes, I could hear him hit the bottom of the step and then he was gone.

I walked up the stairs and headed to the office door and knocked on it. Gabriel opened the door and gave me a hug.

"Look, I am sorry about the conflict with the chick and I am going to head back to the hotel, I just wanted to say good night." I said while he was still hugging me.

"It's not your fault Kensie; you have nothing to apologize about. I am sorry and I apologize on Spencer's behalf because he let it get out of control, he should have had her escorted out as soon as he seen her." Gabriel added.

"You know, I was thinking, right now might not be the best time for me to be here, and believe me, I have had a great time, but I think I might want to go home early, if that would be okay with you to change the return date." I paused, "Some things are meant to be, and some things are not." I said with a heartfelt smile.

"I really wish you would give me another day to make it up to you, but I understand. I will call in the morning to see if I can have it changed but it was set for the return date of Saturday. Please give me another day to make it up to you." He said in his most heartfelt voice.

"I can't, I can't wait that long, I really have to go home. This was a mistake Gabriel, a HUGE mistake." I said as calmly as I could.

"I can't begin to explain how happy I was when you first sent me that friend request, how excited I was that you found me, and I have hardly had time to spend with you and I didn't expect it to be this way. Sometimes I act on a whim and I had no idea everything I was working on would become such a mess." Gabriel paused. "And…" He stopped.

"It's okay; you don't have to say anything else. Let's just sleep it off. I'll call you tomorrow and maybe we can talk then, I can't be responsible for my actions right now, too much has happened." I said as I put my head down.

"Would you want to wait for me, you can lay down in my office on the couch while I close everything up, and then I will take you home…if you want?" Gabriel said and asked at the same time.

"I think I'm just going to head back, I will call a cab; it isn't that big of a deal, that way you don't have to worry about me." I said.

"You sure you will be okay?" Gabriel asked.

"Yes, I'll be fine. Thank you." I gave Gabriel a hug and turned to walk away. By now, I was extremely sober and felt like I could rule the world if I wanted. My anger seemed to be falling out of my ears and I'm sure everyone around me knew it.

Chapter 11-One Moment in Time

I shut the door and headed down the stairs. I didn't want him to follow me out, I was so livid that I didn't want to see him again until tomorrow. He was too busy for me, too busy to fall in love, too busy to hear anything I had to say. When I got outside, someone had hit the fire hydrant down the street from the club, I tried to flag down a cab but there were people in the street and I could hear a siren coming so I thought maybe I should walk down to the next block and then flag a cab.

Josh and Liam were outside the club as I walked past, Liam asked if I wanted a ride and I thanked him for offering but declined. They both looked apologetic and I'm not sure why, the whole thing was my fault anyway for jumping to conclusions, and I probably shouldn't have started drinking that early in the morning. I walked right past the exploding hydrant, it soaked me but I didn't care. I was still hot with anger and it actually felt good. I stood there for a second and put my hands out, *this is my life*, I said out loud. I walked to the next block and tried to flag down the next cab crossing the side street. Spencer drove past and rolled down his window. *Oh Geez*, I thought to myself.

As soon as I seen him, I turned to walk back up the street the club was on, I didn't want to talk to him right now either. I felt bad about everything that happened at the club and I didn't need a reminder of any of it.

He parked on the corner and ran up the street to me, as I starting to get close to the exploding fire hydrant, he grabbed my arm.

"Kensie, I'm so sorry about the situation earlier..." He said as the siren got closer I could barely hear what he was saying but I stopped and we both were soaked. *Did he not realize he was getting drenched?* He looked incredibly hot soaking wet. He had on a long pair of shorts and a polo shirt. I wanted to tell him everything I felt or thought, this moment couldn't have been any perfect, but, I didn't.

"What?" I said to him over the noise.

"I just told Gabriel I'm leaving for Florida in the morning and I wanted to tell you how sorry I am for the horrible evening, and I can't keep apologizing and you not accepting it." He smiled as we moved away from the hydrant.

"I told Gabriel I want him to change my flight home, so I am leaving tomorrow too." I said.

"I, I," Spencer stumbled over his words. I watched him intently wondering what he was going to say. "Your eyelashes are beautiful wet." He said smiling.

"Oh geez, you guys just don't give up, I'm so over both of you." I yelled back.

"I'm serious Kensie, I don't understand why or how your past relationships have led you not to trust or believe in anyone." He said still standing there, soaking wet.

"I don't let people get close to me you jack ass. I don't care anymore." I said turning to walk back down the street.

"That's it, that's exactly it, you're afraid of being left alone again." Spencer said like he understood my entire life.

"How would you know-you know nothing." I said back as I stopped.

"You have no faith because you could never let go of Gabriel, now that you have been around him again, you realize it isn't what you thought it was going to be and now you are afraid he will leave you again." He said as he stood there with his hands on his hips.

"That's not it at all; you have NO clue what I have gone through or how I feel." I said staring at him.

"But I do, my dear, and you think you can't love anyone but Gabriel." He said smiling.

"Is that funny to you? I mean, I'm glad you finally decided to chime in with your psychological ideas." I said back yelling at him.

"Please let me give you a ride home." He finally said.

Josh and Liam were standing directly next to me and were staring right at me. I didn't know what to say. I wanted to yell so loud the entire world heard me. I wanted to yell, *I really don't give two shits anymore.* I turned around and looked Spencer directly in the eyes, and walked up to him.

"You think you can fix this, all this that I have messed up? Sure Spencer, you can give me a ride home." I caved but said with sarcasm.

We walked back to the corner to Spencer's car; he got in the trunk and got out two towels. I tried to shake off some of the water from my hair. Since I wore that damn sheer dress, it just stuck to me like tape. He handed me a towel and opened the passenger side door.

Did I just get in? I put the towel on the seat and got in. He shut the door, got in the driver's side and dried his hair with his towel.

"I gave you that towel to dry off with, not sit on." He laughed.

"I was not about to get in this car all soaking wet. Your seats will get wet." I said as I wiped my wet hair out of my face. "I'm not arguing with you. I'm sorry and I accept your apology." I finally said.

"I don't want to argue with you but I will if I have to, and I really don't know why." He said as he sat there staring at me.

"Let's start this conversation over, what were you saying about going home?" I said trying to stop arguing about arguing.

"I think I need to take a break, I'm sorry about this evening and pretty much your entire trip." Spencer said as he started to drive off.

"If it weren't for you, I wouldn't have had a trip at all; it's weird how things work out. The last seven days, minus this one, have been really great. I wanted to tell Gabriel so badly how long I have loved him, how long I thought about him, but I don't think he has time to hear that and he has enough psycho's in his life, apparently." I smiled.

"Yeah, great left hook, by the way, if I would have known you were going to hit her, I'd been facing you instead of her. I didn't expect it. I didn't want her to hit you, that's why I was facing her." He laughed.

"I don't like confrontation, but she really made me mad, then she knocked you're..." I stopped. "...I haven't drank like that in many years." I laughed.

"I don't want to take you home. I don't want to be alone right now." He said as he turned down the next street.

"I really don't want to be alone either." I said staring back at him meaning it but not meaning it. Part of me wanted to hang out with him and keep listening to things I already knew, and part of me wanted to be alone.

"If you are going home tomorrow, and I am going home tomorrow, we should talk; I don't want it to end like this." He said as he took his towel and rubbed more water off my face.

"I am sorry I jumped to conclusions about this morning at Gabriel's, and I felt like you guys were playing games with me." I said.

"I assure you; neither of us were playing games with you...we both..." and he stopped. "Are you hungry?" He asked me.

"A little, are you?" I asked back.

"Actually, I am, I haven't eaten since lunch." He said.

"All I want right now is a normal meal, like that makes any sense, a hamburger and French fries." I laughed.

"Do you want to go back to my apartment? I will make you anything you want, or we can go to a fast food restaurant, no strings attached." Spencer seemed so serious.

"I really don't feel like going for fast food. I'm soaked." I laughed pointing at my hair.

"Back to the subject, this was not a game, neither one of us planned for any of this to happen, I honestly like you, and I think you are a great person. Gabriel is a wonderful, down to earth person as well; he just has a lot going on in his life." He said.

"Yeah, I can see that, I just hoped things would be so different. It's so ironic that some things you think are one way; really aren't." I said.

"What do you mean by that? He's a real person." He laughed.

"I don't know, I can't explain it." I stopped.

We had been driving for about ten minutes when he pulled up in front of an apartment complex that looked like half doubles sitting next to each other, connected, with stairs leading up to them. They were very nice. He got out and opened my door.

"Oh, I forgot you don't like to have your door opened." He smiled, shut the door-then stepped back five feet.

"It's okay; I'm used to it now. You guys have corrupted every relationship I will have in the future; I will wonder why he isn't opening my door." I laughed as I re-opened the door and got out.

We walked up the stairs and he opened the door. His place was relatively clean, not that I expected different, but it didn't seem like he spent much time there, big surprise.

It was almost like a loft apartment, the living room was huge and the bedroom was an open room above everything. The only thing enclosed was the bathroom with tinted glass. It was a very huge area and you could pretty much see everything. When we walked past the kitchen, he grabbed the clothes he had on at the beach off his kitchen counter and picked up some shoes.

He handed me a towel and headed up the winding steps to his bedroom area. I couldn't take my eyes off him.

I sat at the corner of the couch and dried my hair. I looked around the apartment at all his pictures and the décor wasn't really that of a young single guy. The colors were maroon and hunter green; he had a few candles, and a fireplace.

On each side of the fireplace were built in shelves that had these tall white vases with flowers that matched the walls. The tiles in the fireplace and the floor were maroon and green. Even the curtains matched the walls. He had a huge television. He came back down and handed me a shirt and some sweat shorts, luckily, they had a draw string; they were huge.

"Who decorated your apartment?" I laughed while holding up the shorts to show him how big they were.

"My mom." He said as he went into the kitchen, "Bathroom is right there." He said as he pointed forward.

I went into the bathroom and changed out of my wet clothes, hanging them up in the shower on a towel rack. I messed with my hair for a minute, trying to make it look half way decent but ended up putting it in a pony-tail and folding it under.

My makeup was ruined. I had mascara everywhere. I tried to use toilet paper to get rid of some of it; it didn't really work. When I went into the kitchen, he was frying hamburgers. *Who was this guy? Why wasn't he with someone?*

"I think I have just about everything you might need, check it out and see what you want in the fridge." Spencer said as he pointed to this metal door embedded into the wall but never turned to look at me.

"I just want mustard and pickles, if you have it." I laughed without looking in the fridge.

I watched him turn the hamburgers. He had on a pair of basketball shorts and no shirt, no shoes, no socks. He was so tan, he looked so natural. I tried not to stare at him but if I did, I knew that might make him look at me and I didn't want him to do that at all. I sat on the edge of his couch again, looking around and spotted the stereo.

"Do you need some help?" I asked.

"Nope, you want something to drink?" He said.

"Sure." I said.

He threw me a soda from the fridge and I actually caught it. He laughed. I went over to his stereo and started thumbing through his cd's. He was right; he did listen to everything, just like me. I found one of Sarah McLachlan's cd's.

"May I?" I asked as I held up the cd but kept my head down.

"Sure." He said as he put the burgers on a plate.

I pulled it out and put the cd in. I played 'Angel'.

"I loved this movie. It was so sweet, BUT, not my favorite." I said with excitement.

"I think I heard something earlier about your favorite movie, which is still pretty funny to me, why do you think I waited on you to come out of the club? I mean, I had to make sure, honestly, that it was your favorite movie." He said laughing.

"Why are you laughing? It IS my favorite movie." I said back as I stood in front of the fireplace.

"Out of all the movies in the world, you pick that one, from the 80's, weren't you an infant when that came out?" He smiled.

"So were you, but it's a cute story, you wouldn't know anything about it because you were probably the 'Jake Ryan' to someone at some point in your life." I said never cracking a smile.

"I suppose, a few times." He laughed.

"I also love that fireplace, it's beautiful." I said as got closer to it.

"It isn't real, it glows and you can turn it on, but it doesn't produce heat." He laughed, "Here, I'll turn it on." He said as he came over and turned on a switch.

"Pretty." I said as I started to spin around.

I hadn't heard 'Angel' in forever. Spencer sat on the edge of the couch and watched me, wiping his hands with his kitchen towel.

"Dance with me." I said.

"I don't dance." He laughed as he returned to the kitchen.

Spencer took the fries out of the basket and put them on a plate. He didn't take his eyes off me. I felt so free, so full of life, so comfortable that nothing else mattered.

Not tomorrow, not in the morning, not next week, not my outburst, not Gabriel, not the girl with the black eye. I went into the kitchen and got the condiments out of the fridge.

"So, you're leaving tomorrow?" I asked him trying to make some more conversation.

"Yeah, I haven't been home since last year, my parents haven't been able to visit here in a while, so I really want to see them. Gabriel will be leaving soon and I won't know what to do with myself." He said as he leaned on the counter and laughed.

"It's been a great trip, but I'm ready to go home. I guess I envisioned that I would come here, find what I had been looking for and everything in my crazy fairy tale would come true, but I realized that it doesn't always happen that way. Some things are meant to be, and some aren't." I said handing Spencer some ketchup.

"I can't say I understand it, Gabriel talked about you quite often, sometimes so much I felt like I knew you myself, and everything he said about you was true, how great you were, had a great heart, but I guess this is his way of life. I thought once you got here, things would be different, but this is how it is every day. I guess happiness isn't meant to be on everyone's life agenda. I'm not saying he's not happy, but a different kind of happy." He finished.

"I am so thankful I got to come here, I felt like a kid again on spring break. I really did have a great trip." I said with a smile as I leaned back on his wall.

"I know for a fact that it isn't what you wanted it to be; I know you love him, I know how much you care about him.

I see it in your face." He said looking directly into my eyes, still leaning over the counter.

"I guess I thought it was him, but it really isn't." I said looking him directly in the eyes; then I looked away because I thought I was going to cry.

"Everyone has that somebody, the one we never forget, it's that aching feeling we have when we see them years later, I have that too, there was a girl I dated off and on in high school, when I went home last, I seen her, it hurt, I know how you feel, I don't tell too many people about that, I think she is the reason I have relationship issues, but I'm over it. She broke up with me every other week, it's weird you know, but we have to move on." Spencer said as he stared at me intently.

"I know, I know, but it truly never went away." I said as I finally started to get teary eyed.

As 'Angel' went off, it was silent for a minute and then 'I Will Remember You' played next. Spencer moved the fries and hamburgers to the island in the center of the kitchen and grabbed my hand. He led me into the living room and we began to slow dance. He put his hands on my face and wiped my crazy hair out of it, and the tear that started running down my cheek.

As the song started to play, I thought about every moment we spent together in this short time. I so wanted to tell him that I myself had moved on from Gabriel. I wanted to tell him how incredibly wonderful and caring I thought he was, how I had grown to care about him in such a short period of time, but I knew it would never work. The lyrics played on.

"I will remember you, will you remember me? Don't let your life pass you by, weep not for the memories. Remember all the good times that we had, we let them slip away from us when things got bad, clearly I first saw you, smiling in the sun, I want to feel your warmth upon me, I want to be the one, I will remember you, will you remember me?"

"Isn't that like a best friend, to make everything better when something goes wrong?" I whispered.

He continued to dance with me but didn't say a word as the song continued to play, '*Don't let your life pass you by, weep not for the memories.*' He really could dance. He may have lied a little on that one.

"I didn't think you danced." I said to Spencer.

He didn't say a word; just put his index finger to my mouth in an effort to keep me from talking anymore. He looking at me seriously, deep into my eyes, almost so deep I felt like he could see through my soul, but he never looked away.

It was a bit awkward because he was so much taller than me, but I just pressed my head against his chest. I could hear his heart beating; it seemed so loud-so alive. I started to cry again, praying he didn't notice it. I tried not to listen to it, but it was so strong. He noticed my tears; he tipped my head up and wiped them from my eyes.

As the last chorus played, Spencer kissed me. It was like magic. Magic I had never felt before. I didn't analyze it; I didn't give it a second thought. I kissed him back. We fell to the floor, me on my back and him hovering on top of me, but he had his arms extended out on the floor and the rest of his body was above me, but not touching me. It was completely quiet as the cd playing had stopped. He stayed like that for about five minutes and I was just looking up at him like I didn't know what to do, I didn't know if he expected me to touch him, or if we were going to have sex, I didn't know what to do. He looked me deeply in the eyes, his eyes and mine never left each other. He leaned down and kissed me like I had never been kissed. He didn't kiss me like Gabriel had kissed me, he didn't kiss me like anyone had ever kissed me, he kissed me like he meant it.

His lips were so soft, his eyes were glossy. I had this gorgeous guy posted above me; all I wanted to do was wrap my legs around him. He moved beside me but never stopped kissing my face, my forehead, my neck, I was starting to sweat. I felt like I was going to pass out, I felt like I had heat exhaustion but at the same time, I felt so bad.

Was it because I was leaving and I knew this was it? Just like Gabriel and me, all over again at 15. *Did Gabriel and I's relationship ironically lead me to this?*

He moved from my neck to my chest and I began to feel myself breathe harder and harder. He was breathing harder and harder. He stopped and put his head on my chest and shook his head.

"I can't." He said with a sound of pain in his voice. "We are both heading home tomorrow and I can't let this be it. I just can't." He finished as he rested his head on the left side of my chest…right where my heart was pounding.

"If you hadn't stopped, I would have stopped you." I said back in agreement. "I don't want this to end this way either." I sighed.

I wasn't sure if I would have done anything more with him, believe me, I wanted to. I wanted him to touch me everywhere his hands wanted to go and mine to him, but I knew it was not what I wanted. After all, I still hadn't told Gabriel everything and having sex with Spencer the night before I left California may have made me regret it. We never did eat the hamburgers. We laid there in silence for a short period of time still trying to catch our breaths. He leaned over me and turned off the lights with a remote switch on the coffee table. We both just laid there looking at the sky through the living room window.

"I don't want you to leave, it's late…please stay." He whispered.

"I'm not going anywhere." I said as I smiled at him.

He put his arm around me as I lay on my side. I was facing him and started to rub the inside of his face, he hadn't shaved in a few days so I ran my finger across his stubble. I guess I have this thing about rubbing the inside of guy's faces, but only to the ones I really like. I rubbed the inside of his jaw, then his nose, his eyes, almost like a blind person trying to feel what someone looks like. After a half hour of complete silence, he got up and grabbed some blankets and pillows from this chest that was sitting next to his couch.

"Is this okay?" He asked sweetly.

"Yes." I said quietly holding back my tears and my yearning to tell him how much I wanted to see him again.

He sat back down but this time behind me and put his arm around me. He rubbed the inside of my back with the palm of his hand. I fell asleep shortly after, the plush rug we were laying on was very comfortable.

When I woke up, we were in the exact same spot as we were in when we fell asleep. The first time I have ever had a guy keep his arm around me for an extended period of time. Six hours without either one of us moving. I turned to face him, and for the next hour, I watched him sleep. When I sat up, he rolled from his side to his back. I laid back down on my side, with my elbow on the ground, my hand in my hair. I swept my left hand across the inside of his arm. I traced the outline of his tattoo with my finger. He looked so peaceful.

I wanted to remember that moment forever. I traced his lips gently but not enough to wake him. I put my head on his chest and he put his arm around me. I didn't think he was awake. I listened to his heart beat for at least an hour. I slowly got up, kissed his forehead and went into the kitchen to clean up the mess we made and never ate. I was hoping he didn't wake up. *What would I have said?* I put my own clothes back on and folded the ones that Spencer gave me. I smelled like him, my hair smelled like his cologne. I could still smell it on me. I sat on the edge of his couch and watched him sleep for a bit longer and snuck out slowly so I didn't have to say goodbye. I didn't want to. I went back to the hotel and called my dad.

Chapter 12-Heading Home

"Can you please get me a plane ticket to leave as soon as possible?" I said to my dad as soon as he answered the phone. "Gabriel said he would change the plane ticket but I don't know when he will do it and I want to come home NOW!" I screamed at my dad but didn't know why.

"Are you okay?" He asked.

"I am fine dad; I just want to come home, now." I told him.

"I will call the airline and get the next flight in, I will pick you up at the airport, I love you honey." My dad said trying to console me but didn't ask any more questions.

That's why I talked to my dad and not my mom because she would have turned a five second question into a thirty minute conversation.

I started packing my things. My dad called back and told me that the next available flight was in about six hours. I decided to take one last walk in Santa Monica before I left. I took out my camera and took lots of pictures of random things.

I passed a jewelry store and I looked in the window. I saw my necklace and earrings! I went in to find out how much it was. The tag had $1650 on it.

Had Spencer really spent that much on it? I know we didn't make that much money. I twisted the necklace around and around. NO ONE; and I mean NO ONE ever spent that much money on me on one gift. I wanted to take it back to him, it was too much, but I left in deep thought and found myself on the bus headed to the pier. I needed to clear my mind. I couldn't take it back to him, then I would have to say goodbye and it was already bad enough.

What was wrong with me? I needed to stop second guessing myself. I was still the same person I always was. I decided to call Gabriel. He had left a few messages for me since I had talked to him last night.

"Gabriel, I had my dad book a flight back to Tennessee, I wanted to meet up with you and say goodbye before I left; I've got about an hour or so." I said.

"Where are you? I can meet you now." He said.

"I'm at the pier." I replied.

"Give me ten minutes and I will be there." He said.

I hung up the phone and sat on the edge of the beach. About fifteen minutes later I seen Gabriel's car pull up. I got up to walk over to him as he got out. I thought to myself, *this is the first time since I've been here that he dropped everything he was doing to be with me.* He had his hands in his pockets and had a sad look on his face. I saw that face once, the day I got into my dad's car and left Florida for good.

"I tried to call you last night after you left." He said.

"I…" Gabriel stopped me.

"Just let me finish…" He said as he walked around his car closer to me. "I know that when we started emailing each other, it was weird. It was feelings I hadn't dealt with in years. I know that we always said we would be friends and I don't want that to change. I love you, always have, always will, but I don't have time in my life right now for the love you want from me. I wish I could, I know that no one ever smiled at me like you do, or did, no one ever made me laugh like you did. I hope you will forgive me for what I have become, for how I have acted, I can't say anymore it wasn't the right timing, maybe it was. You seemed to give up on what you thought was real, what you believed in. I started to think about what you said about things being meant to be, you are right. We went through a lot when we were young, I was there when you scraped your knees on the dock the last time I seen you, when your grandmother died, I was there when you caught your first fish, seeing you again brought me happiness and lots of good memories." He said while pausing.

"Time doesn't wait on us Gabriel, we wait on time. Now that I am here, it doesn't make me happy. It almost feels like I'm in the way, causing problems for everyone, disrupting your life." I said with tears in my eyes. "Do you know what I wanted to tell you? I wanted to tell you that I never stopped thinking about you, I had the hugest crush on you, and I loved you so bad that it almost killed me when I left Florida. When I started doing therapy, I spent so much time trying to get myself out of my depression that I wrote you a hundred times but never mailed them. You never forget your first true love, it never dies. My whole life I have looked for someone like you, comparing them to you, my whole outlook on what love was supposed to be revolved around what I felt when I was with you, maybe in another world it is real, but not in this one, not now." I began to cry harder.

"I know all of that; you don't think it didn't kill me? That I didn't feel too? I had one best friend, you. I shouldn't have let you leave without staying in touch, and I understand why you didn't, but I should have pushed to keep you in my life. I can only imagine where we would be today. I know that I should have done things different, and I am sorry for that, but… I talked to Spencer this morning…" He paused.

Great, Spencer probably told him I stayed with him last night, I did not want to end my relationship with Gabriel this way, but I didn't know what to say anymore.

"He's packing to go home today for a few weeks, I don't think you should give up on yourself, or love. He loves you Kensie, I know it, I feel it, and he has never loved anything the entire time I have known him but his family and his car. He gave his car to Josh to watch over instead of parking it at my house while he was gone. MY jaw had to have hit the floor and bounced back a hundred times when I heard that. His car is like his kid. He said last night he listened to you breathe while you slept for hours. That's love. He told me he fell in love with you the very first conversation he had with you. I love you, but he is in love with you. I hear it in his voice. I don't want you to stop believing in love because we are different people now." He finished.

"Why didn't he say something yesterday?" I asked him.

"Kensie, you are not naive, you know men don't think like that. We don't want women to know what we think or feel. He's my best friend and I know him better than he knows himself. He doesn't just fall in love on a whim, probably why he never had a stable relationship. I'm not going to be mad at you for wanting to feel, or be mad at him; I want everyone to be happy. I am happy that my life helped lead you to him, I'm not saying you are going to fall madly in love and get married and all that business, maybe you will, I don't know, you may not even be able to maintain a relationship, or maybe you will…" Gabriel said as a single tear came out of his eye. "But, unknowingly, fate might have paired us up a long time ago for this to happen now, it all happens for a reason Kensie, don't walk away from it." He finished.

I felt so bad, I felt like a lost dog.

"I wish you the best Gabriel." I said as I gave him an intense hug." I hope that you will always stay in touch with me." I said as I let go.

"You are always welcome here, any time you need to get away, or anything you need for that matter. You have my number and I will always answer." He said as he gave me a beautiful smile with tears in his eyes.

He gave me another hug and as he got into his car, I stopped him. I opened my purse and handed him the poem/song I had written.

"This is what I felt, all those years, and now, after this, I thank you, I can finally let go." I smiled.

"I will always love you K, I hope you know that." He said as he took the paper and looked down at it. I'm not sure if he read it right then, but I recited the words over and over in my head as I walked away...

As I walk alone, with no place to go,
The breeze blows past my face-
My tears-they fall like rain,
In no amount of time or space.
Just an open field-with no place to hide-
The path I walk down-seems long and wide...
Without you...I'm not me.
Can I run away,
So far away that no one would ever find-
A past that I once loved,
And thought that I could leave behind.
Not a day, not a night, passes,
That I can't see-
What has become,
What I can't be...
Without you...I'm not me.
Lost in silence,
I know I've been here before-
The pain and heartache,
I always said I didn't want anymore
The one thing that overcomes me,
My one biggest fear-
Is something I can't cover up,
It's being here...
Without you...I'm not me.

As he drove away, I cried, and cried, and cried. I didn't care that I cried. I didn't care that I just spilled my heart out to someone I no longer knew.

Every memory I had of him came running through my mind, and what seemed like out the other side and back again. Now this all seemed so minor. I wiped the tears from

my eyes and walked up to the area where the bus would be.
I cried some more.

I had a torn feeling in my soul, *what if I had given it a
chance and made him realize we could have had something
great? Does he kiss all of his best friends like that? He had
to feel something for me or he wouldn't have done that?
Right?* Then I realized; you can't change someone. You
can't change what someone has become; you can only hope
they might find their way home somehow. I realized he
wasn't coming home.

I decided to go get my things from the hotel and get a cab
to the airport a little early. I sat in the terminal balling my
eyes out. I felt like my heart was ripped from my chest.

Should I call Spencer? I thought. I never really said
goodbye and I kind of yelled at him about that.

Immediately everything Gabriel said to me came to mind,
but it was probably best if I just let it go, all of it. Although
I refrained from calling him, I did look around the terminal
to see if he might have been there, heading home. I got on
my plane and felt exactly how I didn't want to feel, what
might have been. *Could I have actually loved someone that
much?* It really wasn't Gabriel, just as I suspected, maybe it
was just the feeling of love that I missed. I put in my ear
phones and hit shuffle on my phone attempting to use music
to block out everyone around me talking,

That was the longest plane flight I have ever taken. I don't
know what I was thinking, even if Gabriel and I had
connected again, my girls would never accept it, I had
nothing to offer him, there I was, analyzing again. I couldn't
sleep the flight off, I tried.

I thought maybe I would return to normal when I got
home and this was probably just a phase. When my plane
landed, my dad was right there to pick me up; right on time.
I told him about my trip but it was mostly silent.

"We all chase dreams lady bug." My dad used the nick
name he hadn't called me in years. "Some of those dreams
we know from the beginning weren't even real. It's a part of
life." My dad said in a dad kind of way.

"It wasn't really a dream I was chasing, it was, nothing. I don't want to talk about it anymore." I said as I fought to hold back my tears.

I put my ear phones back in and my dad knew that I was not going to talk about it anymore no matter what he said. I had no idea that my whole world was about to come crashing down on me. As we took that twenty minute drive home, I just stared out the window. My dad patted me on the head like he did when I was a girl. As one love song ended, another one played. Fergie's 'Big Girls Don't Cry' came on and I nearly lost it. *Could this song have been any more of a way to explain how I felt?*

It was one song for both of them. Damn music, damn my life, damn the shitty hand I got dealt. As the words played, I could feel the tears rolling down my cheeks, but I kept my head turned to the right so my dad wouldn't see me crying.

'The smell of your skin lingers on me now, you're probably on your flight back to your home town, I need some shelter of my own protection baby, to be with myself...' I knew I should have shuffled through that song; but I didn't.

'...Fairy tales don't always have a happy ending, do they...' the song continued on. I could still smell Spencer's cologne in my hair, as the breeze blew in my dad's window; I tried so hard not to show him I was hurting. This song was about both of them rolled into one, just like I had told Nora; I wished I could roll them into one person. I knew I would NEVER hear this song again and not think of my trip to Santa Monica.

As the next part of the song played, *'...But it's time for me to go home, it's getting late...'* I honestly didn't know why I let myself keep listening to it, it was the most perfect song, every word made me hurt even more.

I shut my phone off so I didn't have to hear anymore. My dad pulled up in front of my house, which I thought was odd because the girls were at their house. I sat there looking at my cute, tiny house.

My dad got out of the car and opened my car door. I tried to wipe the tears from my eyes; I knew he had to have known I was crying. My eyes were probably light brown by now.

"I have some bad news lady bug." My dad said as he got my things out of the back seat.

I thought what now? Can it get any worse?

"What?" I said as I walked up the steps and got my key out.

"Cairo…" He stopped.

"What about Cairo?" I yelled knowing it wasn't good.

"He got out of the garage a few days ago and was hit by a car. I'm so sorry Kensie, I really, really am." My dad's eyes filled with tears.

I immediately dropped my keys and purse, put my hand over my mouth to hide the scream, and dropped to my knees. My dad helped me up and we walked around the back of the yard where he had buried him and made a little sign that said "CAIRO" and I lost it all.

"Do the girls know?" I managed to get out in 3 breaths.

"Yes, I told them this morning. Your mother had them at the store the day it happened. Your mom was a mess. She wanted to tell you but I told her not to ruin your vacation." My dad said with tears running down his face. I rarely ever seen my burly father cry; and if I did, it was something really bad.

I came back feeling worse than I did when I left, and my dog died.

"Lady bug; I really am sorry, come get the girls when you are ready." He said as he turned to walk back out to the street.

I sat on my back porch steps waiting for him to come running up to me with his goofy little ears and wagging tail. I waited for him to come to me like he did last week. I sat there until it got dark crying. When I stood up I was lightheaded but I managed to make my way over to his dog house and kicked it saying, "Stupid life, stupid, it's all stupid." I suddenly knew the outburst wouldn't make it better and I knew I had to get it together because I had to go get my girls.

I went into the house, changed into some shorts and a tee shirt, hooked my camera up to my computer, downloaded all my pictures and sent them to my mom. I looked through them briefly but I kept looking at the picture of the girls and Cairo I had hanging up on the wall next to my computer. I began to cry again and put my head down on the desk. The wood desk began to soak up my tears and I cried so hard my eyes were blurry and I started shaking.

It was like I just took a class in depression 101 and how to do it right. I drove over to my parent's house and my girls came running out to me.

"Mommy, Cairo got hit by a car and papaw said the lady was crying and she said she was sorry, do you forgive her?" Marie asked.

"I do, it wasn't her fault honey." I said as I held back the tears.

"Did you have fun mommy?" Rayanne asked.

"Yes, and I took lots of pictures but not as many as I should have because I forgot my camera at the hotel a couple of times I was out." I said as I grabbed both my girls' hands.

"If there is ever anything in your life that you want to do, don't ever let anyone or anything stop you from doing it. One day it might be too late to do it." I told them both.

My mother told the girls to go play upstairs in my old room, which was their converted play room and took my hands and led me into her bedroom.

"I'm so sorry about Cairo. It happened a few days ago and I didn't want to tell you until you got back." My mother said.

I lost it again.

"I know he meant the world to you." She continued.

"It's not just that, I had the most confusing trip I have ever taken and then I come home to this." I said with big tears running down my face.

I explained everything to my mom; we were in there for at least an hour. Spencer to Gabrielle, she heard it all.

"Well, honey, your father and I have been together for a very long time, we love each other very much, and that's epic enough for me. I guess everyone views love differently. My meeting him was the greatest thing that ever happened to me. You should go home, and call Spencer. We weren't expecting you back until the morning anyway, so go home, get some sleep and we will see you at church in the morning. I want to take the girls to the fair after church anyway, so you can have the day off after the play. I really don't mind, they have been pretty good and I'm going to miss them not being here all day and night." My mother said with a tear in her eye.

"I love you." I told my mother as I hugged her.

I kissed the girls and told them I would see them in the morning. After considerable pondering and a lot of self-conditioning, I went home and called Spencer.

"Hello?" A guy said and it wasn't Spencer.

"Um, hello, I'm trying to reach Spencer?" I said.

"Oh, he's not here, I'm his cousin." He said.

"Okay, can you please have him call Kensie when he gets in?" I asked.

"Kensie?" He repeated my name.

"Yes, thank you." I said.

After I hung up the phone, I fell asleep on my bed, wishing Cairo was lying there with me. I was sad but my eyes hurt from all the crying I had done but I couldn't bring myself to crying anymore.

I got up the next morning and went to church with my parents and the girls. They did wonderful in their play and I was glad I got to see it. My mom came up to me later and handed me an envelope.

"Do what you have to do. Don't worry about it, I enjoy having the girls. Besides, it isn't that far." She said.

I opened the envelope and it was a plane ticket to Florida, for…today.

"Mom, I don't understand." I said.

"Don't play cutesy with me, Kensie, you know darn good and well what you need to do. Your father and I have spent more money in plane tickets in the last day than we want to for the next year. Look at it as an early birthday present." She smiled.

"I still don't get it; I'm back to square one again." I said.

"Gabriel called me last night; he sounds like the same sweet boy." She said. "I got Spencer's parent's address from him, it's written down on the back of the envelope." She finished as short as she could be.

"Gabriel called you?" I asked surprised.

"He said he knew you weren't going to do anything about it, and he knew Spencer wouldn't either so he called us to make sure that you two met up again. He said he didn't want you to wait fifteen more years." She smiled. "Spencer sounds to me like a wonderful person; you might not want to mess this one up." She said.

"How, why? How am I going to mess this up?" I said.

"The ticket has an open return date so just call the airline and find out about return flights when you are ready to come home." She said.

My dad gave me a nod and instead of arguing with her, I thanked her. *Did they want me to fly to Florida to meet up with Spencer?* He hadn't even called me back. Let's see, in the last week, I managed to meet up with Gabriel and now they wanted me to go back to Florida to find Spencer? *What is wrong with them?* I thought to myself but I figured it was worth a try. I did owe him a proper goodbye.

So I got in my car and drove to the airport. I was in such deep thought that I didn't even turn the radio on. I'm glad my parents had some extra money saved up because I had drained my savings. Wait! I had to work on Monday. Maybe I could take an extended vacation day. Inside the envelope was a gift card to rent a car to drive while I was in Florida. On the back was Spencer's parent's address and phone number.

I had no idea what I was going to say, or do, but for some reason, it seemed right.

Chapter 13-Back to Florida

When I got on the plane, I did nothing but think of how ignorant this was, how silly he was going to think I was, *what if Gabriel was wrong? What if he had no desire to see me?* The hour and a half flight didn't really seem that long. When I got off the plane, I used the internet on my phone to find driving directions to Spencer's parent's house. I rented a car and made the drive to Sarasota. All the sights were running back to me and I remembered when my grandmother drove me back one summer and we had a flat tire on the highway.

The directions to his parent's house was exactly how I remembered going to my grandmothers, it had just been so long and I was so young I didn't know the street names. I found the street they lived on but I circled around the block and went a block over to pass by my grandmother's old house. It was a different color now, I wanted to get out and walk into their back yard and see if that old dock was still there to the channel.

I ended up stopping for a few seconds, thinking about Gabriel and my grandmother, how she used to have a double swing in the front yard, the swing was now gone.

I nervously drove back over to Spencer's parent's house. I parked in their drive and walked up to knock on the door.

"Hello?" A lady answered.

"Hello, my name is Kensie Newman and I'm looking for Spencer?" I asked.

"He isn't here honey. He left very early this morning." She said as she smiled. He kind of looked like her.

"Hello." I heard a voice say behind her.

"Hello." I said as I shook his mother's hand, then his father's.

"I'm Spencer's dad, Blaine, his mother Amelia." He said as he finished shaking my hand. Spencer looked just like his dad, it was uncanny.

"This is Kensie." His mother said like they knew me.

"My you have gotten big!" His father said.

"I'm sorry?" I said without thinking. I was confused.

"I did some work for your grandfather a long time ago, you were just a girl then, it was way before he passed away, well, and way before your grandmother." He replied.

"Oh, I'm sorry, I wasn't sure if we had met before and I didn't remember." I said smiling.

"Would you like to come in?" His mother asked as she opened the door and stepped to the side.

"Well, I was just wondering when you might expect him back." I questioned.

"I'm not sure really. I know he rented a car last night and said he was going to Orlando to visit Eli but I don't know if he intended to do that today, he left his phone on his dresser or I'd call him." His mother said laughing.

"Come in." His dad insisted.

I went in and we sat down in the living room. There were pictures everywhere. I couldn't help but look at them as Spencer's parents were talking to me about my grandfather and what a good man he was. There were pictures of Spencer from a baby to graduation. He must have been one hell of an athlete because most of the gazillion trophies in the living room were his.

He was really cute. It all came back to me when I saw one of him at about 7, I did remember seeing him with his dad outside my grandmothers once. It was long ago, maybe it wasn't him at all, I couldn't remember.

"Spencer said he met you, and that you had gone to California to visit Gabriel." His dad said.

"I did, ironic we were in the same area and never really knew each other." I said.

"We didn't let him travel too far, we both worked a lot and he was with a sitter often when he was younger." His dad offered.

His parent's went on and on about him to the point of it being sickening. They did raise a good kid, but I still felt really strange being there, even without him there, even if he were there.

"Would you like to stay for a while?" His mother asked me.

"I guess it would be pointless to call him." I laughed.

"We would love to have you for dinner, if you are hungry." His mother said.

"You know, I actually am, it's been a few days since I have eaten; it surprises me that I'm still standing." I said.

I went outside and called the air-line to book the plane flight back for early in the morning. I called my mom and told her he wasn't there but I was going to wait for him for a while and if he didn't show up, I would stay at the airport until morning and take the next flight out so I didn't have to pay for another day of car rental. I went back into the house and sat down at the kitchen table.

"Can I help you with anything?" I asked his mother.

"Well, you can cut up lettuce for salad, if you'd like." She said as she handed me a bowl and a knife.

"So, is Spencer an only child?" I said as I took the knife from her and began cutting the lettuce.

"He has a younger sister, she is 23, and she lives here, in town." His mother said as she took a picture off the wall of her.

"Pretty, she looks a bit like Spencer, more so like you." I smiled as I handed the picture back to her.

"Do you expect him to come back tonight?" I asked her.

"I'm not sure; he was here for about three hours, had his dad take him to rent a car and then left early. I didn't even know he left his phone here until I heard it ringing earlier." She said. "So, Spencer tells me you have two girls, I couldn't have imagined having two of them. One was bad enough." She laughed.

I felt strange talking to her but I was an out-going person and I could talk to anyone so it wasn't so bad. They must be somewhat normal, they knew my grandpa.

"Yes, I have two daughters, Marie and Rayanne. They are a handful." I said as I grabbed a tomato and started to cut it.

"Blaine is making sirloin on the grill; I hope that is okay with you?" She asked.

"You do not know how okay that is with me." I laughed. "I didn't eat much meat while I was in California.

"They eat a lot of fish, and salads, I noticed when we visited last. We eat a lot of Halibut, but I love my red meat!" She exclaimed.

"Oh, me too, I could barely stand it when we went out to eat, I just followed their lead." I laughed.

"Your grandfather was a good man. Your grandma was a good woman." She paused. "Everyone in this area used to be pretty close a long time ago, my how things have changed. Everyone used to get together and have a big cook out at the beginning of the summer and again in the fall at the park." She finished.

"You know, I remember that, I think it was before my gramps passed though. Grandma didn't do much after he passed away." I said as I handed her the salad bowl.

"That was a sad situation, your grandfather passing away so abruptly." She noted.

"I thought Spencer told me he had a lab?" I asked. "I haven't seen him." I added.

"He took him with him." She said.

"When I got back from vacation, I found out my dog had gotten hit by a car, it was not a good day." I said with sadness.

"Oh my, I'm so sorry to hear that. I think Spencer would be devastated if anything ever happened to Dugger." She said.

"He never told me his name, cute." I said.

Spencer's dad brought in the steaks and we sat down to eat. It was getting dark. His parents were telling me stories about him when he was a kid. Oh he would probably kill them because I would kill my parents if the role was reversed. After we ate, I roamed around the living room and hall for a bit looking at all the pictures.

"I know it's getting late, I didn't know if you were planning on leaving tonight, or if you were going to wait for him. I wish I knew when he was coming home. Do you want to stay here tonight? He might come home and I'd hate for you to miss him." His mother said as she smiled. She had the same dimple Spencer had, just on the other side.

"I would like to stay, it's better than going to the airport until morning. That was my original plan." I told her.

She showed me Spencer's room, there were more trophies everywhere and pictures of him and his friends in his room. His phone rang; his mother hit the end button to shut it up. She told me I could sleep in his room for the night and she was sure he wouldn't mind.

"Thank you, I greatly appreciate it." I thanked her.

"You're welcome honey, any time you are in this area, let us know." She said and gave me a hug.

Why was his mom hugging me? She was really nice but it was a bit odd. *Did he say something to them when he came home?* They acted like they knew more than I did and I just wanted to know what they knew.

"I'm not sure what time you will be up, but I will leave around 8:00 so I can return the car I rented and catch my plane." I told her.

"I would imagine I will be up, but if not, it was wonderful to meet you and I sincerely hope he comes home tonight." She said.

After she left the room, I looked at all his pictures on the dresser, most of them were of his family, his sister, who did look exactly like his mom, and then there were several pictures of his basketball and baseball teams. There were a few pictures of a younger boy, I'm imagining it was Eli because he had several of them with Spencer when Spencer was younger, I'd guess around sixteen.

Behind one of the basketball team pictures was a picture of him, Gabriel, and some girl in the middle. They looked like they were around fifteen, probably taken not much longer after I had seen him last. His phone started to ring again. I walked over to his dresser and picked it up. The phone flashed 'Amanda'. Of course I didn't answer it, but when it stopped ringing, a picture of Ethan popped up. How sweet for him to have a picture of Ethan on his phone. I attempted to shut his phone off. I wanted to look through it so badly but I didn't. It was a pretty fancy phone, and I finally figured out how to shut it off.

I called Nora.

"What are you now doing in Florida?" She asked as I briefly explained to her my new found trip.

"I'm not sure really, but Gabriel told my mom to make sure I didn't wait fifteen years to find Spencer and I felt like he might have been right." I said.

"Girl, you are crazy. Are you going to call me next week from London?" She laughed.

"Hardly doubt it." I told her. "I have to go back to work." I laughed.

We talked for a short while and I told her we were going to have to do lunch sometime soon so we could chat face to face. After we got off the phone, I turned off the light and laid there in his bed, in the dark. I felt a bit strange, almost psychotic like, but his parents invited me, and although I was uneasy about the situation, I listened to every sound.

If I heard something, I wondered if it were him coming home, maybe a dog barking, a car door, anything. On the mirror was a faint glow from star stickers he probably put on there when he was a kid. I set my alarm for 7 on my phone and fell asleep.

When I woke up, I had to pee so badly but I was uncomfortable about walking around in their house. His mom had showed me where everything was but it still felt strange. I opened the door and there was a note taped to the door, it was from his mom. She said to help myself to some coffee, and she hoped to see me again soon. Since no one was home, I did use the bathroom, made myself look half way decent, made Spencer's bed, left her a note at the bottom of hers thanking them for their hospitality, and grabbed some coffee.

After I left their house, I went to the channel where Gabriel and I had spent a lot of time when we were younger. This became my breaking point; the point of no return, the point of everything that had happened since I left Florida at 15. I took out the baggie I had put the ashes in. I thought long and hard about what was once written on the piece of paper I carried with me...the one that was now nothing more than ashes. Those words haunted me. I bent over the channel and slowly put my hand into the baggie. I squeezed the ashes tightly. As I pulled my hand out, I leaned farther into the channel. I extended my arm, released my closed hand, and the wind blew the ashes out of it. A sigh of relief, a tear slowly ran down my cheek and plopped into the ocean. There goes my tear; floating away with those ashes into the ocean current.

I put the baggie into the channel to fill it with water so the rest of the ashes would blend in. I tipped it upside down like it was a bucket, the memories of Gabriel and I making sand castles was the only thing left in my mind. As I stood up I let the breeze run through my hair, shut my eyes and held my hands out to the side. I had wished it were raining because if it were to have been, I would have danced In it and spun around in a circle. I just said goodbye to everything I had ever known about love. The tears I cried weren't for sorrow; they were for something I never knew I had within me, the point of realizing how strong I really was. I turned around and walked away, took a deep breath then got back in the car. *"Never look back if you are truly saying goodbye because that memory will just cloud the reasons why you were there to begin with."* I said out loud. I didn't look back; I just drove to the airport. Well, this was a wasted trip, at least I tried. I was disappointed but I knew if it were meant to be, it would be. I felt a bit better about the letter, closure, and saying goodbye.

Chapter 14-Careful What You Wish For

After I landed, I got my car from the parking spot where I left it, which took up most of my gift card to pay for. Leaving your car at the airport is not cheap, even overnight. On my drive home, I did not listen to my love playlist; I listened to some classic rock. I tried to put everything behind me, including the fact that I had to go home and probably should call work and tell them I would be back in tomorrow. I forgot to call in this morning. Oh well, who cares. It will all be normal again soon.

When I got to my parent's house, no one was there. They didn't leave me a note so I drove home. When I pulled up, both my girls came running out to greet me.

"Are you done leaving yet, mommy?" Rayanne asked me.

"Yes, I'm done leaving." I smiled.

My mom was sitting on the front porch smiling.

"Well, how did it go?" She asked.

"He never came home." I laughed. "It's okay, just another addition to my wonderful week."

"Work called, you didn't call in. I took care of it for you, I told your boss your flight was delayed." She said.

"Thanks, I kind of forgot about that." I said as I rolled my eyes.

My dad came out of the house and stood in front of the door.

"Did you stay at the airport terminal all night?" He asked.

"No, I stayed at Spencer's parent's house. That was strange but they are really nice people." I said.

"His dad, Blaine, used to help your grandfather with the yard and repairs when you were younger." Mom said. "I didn't put two and two together until..." Suddenly my dad leaned over and hit my mom in the arm.

I looked at them very confused.

"Until what, Gabriel called and gave you the rundown of my last week?" I laughed.

I walked up on the porch and gave my dad a hug. He hugged me back tightly and stepped to the side. Everyone was silent, I just looked at all of them because everyone seemed to be up to something.

"What?" I finally asked. I heard Rayanne snicker and I turned around and she quickly covered her mouth with her hand.

"WHAT?" I asked again growing impatient with the silent treatment. My dad pointed to the right. I looked into my front door and seen a dog pacing back and forth. My dad smiled.

"That dog is not replacing Cairo." I said as I opened the screen door and bent down to pet it.

"But you sure are pretty though." I said as I made goofy baby talk noises to the dog. He just kept lapping my face with his tongue.

Spencer stepped out from behind the wall and I could do nothing but stare at him. He stared back. I started crying. He held out his hands and I ran through my living room and jumped up in his arms. He was so much taller than me. He wiped the tears from my eyes and kissed my nose.

"What are you doing here?" I said as I trembled. I was okay at his parents because I didn't think he was going to come home.

"I've been here since late last night. You called your mom a couple of hours before I got here and she said you were coming back today. I told her not to call you and tell you I was here, I wanted it to be a surprise. I drove from Sarasota, Gabriel gave me your parent's address and we came here." He smiled as he pointed to Duggar, my parent's...and my girls.

"I slept in your bed." I said.

"I slept in your bed." He said.

"What did you talk to my parent's about?" I asked.

"What did you talk to my parent's about?" He asked.

"I didn't use your toothbrush." I said as I wiped toothpaste from the side of his mouth.

"I didn't use your toothbrush, I brought mine." He laughed.

I turned around to look at my parent's and my girls. Everyone was staring at me, like I was supposed to say something amazing. All I could do was stare back at Spencer. He was in my living room, in the flesh.

"I can't believe you flew to Sarasota to see me." He said.

"I can't believe you drove all those hours to see me." I said. "I didn't say goodbye, I couldn't. I...I sat there and watched you sleep but couldn't say goodbye." I said.

My parent's turned to take the girls outside so we could talk privately and my father smiled with approval.

"I was glad you didn't wake me, when I woke up and you were gone, I had no idea what I would have said to you but I didn't want you to leave. I called Gabriel and as odd as it was, he gave me some good advice." Spencer smiled.

"I guess he gave my parent's some too because they were the ones who bought the plane ticket for me to come see you." I smiled back.

"For some reason, I can't walk away from you. You have left a dent in my heart." He smiled

"Calro died while I was gone. I was heartbroken; it just got worse and worse." I said sadly.

"Your dad told me." He said as he held me. "Your parent's are great." He said.

"Your parent's are too." I said back.

"I kind of told them all about you when I got there. I accidently left my phone or I would have called but I didn't know that you were going to fly there until I got here, my heart was racing." He admitted.

Was this an admission of a male feeling? I was still shaking.

"So you came here to give me a proper goodbye? Because you promised you would?" I said as I looked up at him with my hands clenched to his shirt.

"Did you fly to Florida to give me a proper goodbye because you made me promise I wouldn't walk away without saying goodbye?" He said back.

"I, I guess I…" I stuttered.

"I came here to say hello." He said smiling down at me as he cut my sentence off.

"I don't want you to leave." I said as I started crying again.

"I don't want to leave." He said.

He grabbed my hands and led me through the living room. We walked out to the porch and he shook my dad's hand. My mom looked at me with tears in her eyes, how could they possibly know what this felt like to me? They were old, maybe they had a story too, and I just didn't know it.

"Spencer, watch this…" Marie said as she did a cart wheel.

"Good job!" He said. "Girls are definitely different than boys. Ethan is so quiet, they are a handful." He smiled.

"I told you they were bad." I said as I wondered if he would be able to deal with them; single guy, used to dealing with a single boy who was almost perfect.

"I love them." He said back as he put his arm around me.

I just kept thinking; *how were they going to react to him?*

"They wouldn't leave me alone. It was fun though, it was late when I got here but we all came over to your house and they showed me around, their room, your bedroom, it was funny because Marie said, 'only mommy goes in there so

STAY OUT!' she yelled at the top of her lungs. They really have been great." He smiled.

Apparently while I was at his parent's thumbing through his pictures in his room, they were blending in with him.

"Spencer, Spencer, watch this!" Rayanne said as she did a hand stand.

"I see you; that's awesome." He said as he walked off the front porch and down to the sidewalk.

He called both girls over to him and was whispering something to both of them.

"He got along great with them Kensie, I think they like him." My dad said. "I wouldn't give you an approval if I didn't feel it in my heart." My dad said.

"Mommy, Spencer said we can go to the park, can we go now, can we?" Rayanne came up and asked me.

"Yeah, can we, please, can we?" Marie chimed in.

"Yes, we can go to the park." I smiled at them, then at Spencer.

Had my dream come true behind my own back? As soon as I shut my eyes and stopped looking for it, it happened. I fought my whole life to find this feeling, and this time, it wasn't just a feeling, it was him.

It was Spencer, someone I would have never guessed I would have ended up falling in love with. Did I think for two seconds that guy I met in my office building and shook my hand with the ball cap and sunglasses on would hold my heart in his hands?

"I guess your dad and I are going to head home." My mom whispered.

"I love you lady bug." My dad said giving me a huge dad hug.

Spencer was helping the girls into my car while I said goodbye to mom and dad.

"Thank you, the both of you. I appreciate everything you have done." I smiled.

"I will kind of miss them, they really weren't that bad. It's been awhile since I have had to give baths every night and put a little girl in bed." She smiled.

"You know, you can have them whenever you want." I laughed.

I got into the car and we drove to the park, Spencer held my hand the entire way.

"I'm not used to having a girl drive me around." He laughed.

"You can drive if it makes you more comfortable." I laughed back squeezing his hand. "Do I have to get out and open your door?" I laughed.

He just smiled; his dimple was so cute I wanted to poke my finger in it. When we got to the park, he helped Marie out of the car and I helped Rayanne. I could tell he was growing attached to her.

"Push us Spencer, push us." They both screamed.

"I'm not sure how this is going to work out with our distance, but I don't want to lose this." Spencer said after he finished pushing Rayanne on the swing.

"I don't want it to end either." I smiled at him.

"I'd like to stay for a few days, if you don't mind. Then I really do have to get back to Florida to visit my mom and my sister." He said.

"I'd like for you to stay, but things aren't like they were in California, I can't just up and leave when I want, the girls are a major part of my life, and…I have to go back to work tomorrow." I said.

"I know, and I am willing to accept that. I can do some sightseeing, there is a lot in Nashville that I would like to do; the role has been reversed." He said as he put his arm around me while we sat on a park bench.

"Mommy likes a boy, mommy likes a boy; mommy likes a boy." Rayanne started singing as they both jumped out of the swing.

"Mommy and Spencer sitting in a tree…" Marie added.

"Stop it, go play." I said to both of them. They giggled and ran off.

"It might take a while for them to get used to it, they aren't used to seeing me with anyone. I haven't dated anyone since my divorce." I laughed.

"They will be fine, it's cute; they are cute." He smiled.

I looked around at the park and seen all the couples holding hands and laughing, and for the first time in a long time, I actually wasn't the one sitting on the bench crying because I longed for that.

I was part of that group now, part of the people I used to watch happy, that was me. I grabbed Spencer's hand to hold it and squeezed it tightly.

"Horseback riding, must be a first." He said.

"I got that, Nora has horses. When you're ready, I'll make one phone call." I smiled.

"By the way, your necklace looks great on you…about that…" He said and stopped.

"About what?" I said as I twisted it around my neck.

"I kind of did spend my money on it too…I just didn't tell Gabriel that. I didn't want him to get mad, but when I saw it, I had to get it for you. I have to be honest." He said. "I never bought a girl anything but flowers in my life so I hope you like it." He finished.

"I love it, I will wear it forever." I said but I didn't tell him I knew how much it cost.

"I know you can't make the trip to Cali whenever you want, so I will do my best in down time to come see you, once Gabriel comes back in a few weeks, we will be really busy, but then it will calm down until he finds something else to do." He said.

"I'm willing to wait, as long as you don't forget me." I said.

"How am I going to do that?" He laughed. "You tell me how I am going to forget you." He smiled.

"It happens. Sometimes things are good for me, then the person just falls off, I notice it happens when it's a full moon, things are great for a few days, them bam, out of nowhere, they just stop talking to me, like the tide changed or something." I said.

"It isn't a full moon." He said seriously.

"Yeah, I guess it isn't." I smiled.

"Quite analyzing me." He said seriously. "I have no intentions but to be with you…hopefully for a long time." He looked down at me with his bright hazel eyes; they were so beautiful with the sun shining on them. No sunglasses today. He was squinting but the colors of his eyes were miraculous.

"Yeah, yeah, I hear ya." I laughed.

"I'm serious; you have to stop doing that." He said seriously.

"Did you bring any clothes?" I changed the subject.

"I did. I put my stuff in your dresser." He stopped. "I'm just kidding. I thought about doing that as a joke but I didn't know how you would re act so it's in my car." He laughed.

"Your mom said you were there for a few hours and left. Did you call them and tell them where you were?" I asked.

"They knew where I was going." He smiled.

"She said you went to Orlando." I said back.

"I told her I was stopping there first, but she knew where I was going after that. I stopped to see Eli, played some basketball, met up with some of his friends, took a nap, I then just drove. I stopped at few places along the way. It's been awhile since I took a road trip." He smiled.

"Why did they ask me to stay if they knew you weren't coming back?" I said.

"Because they knew you probably weren't going to be able to get a flight directly back, and I told them about you so they wanted to spend some time with you." He said.

"We ate steak." I laughed. "It was wonderful." I smiled.

"Oh, thanks for cleaning up that mess we made in the kitchen before you left, I got up and was like, what the? Oh, well, glad she cleaned the kitchen and didn't wake me up to say goodbye." He laughed.

"I wasn't going to leave it like that." I said as I hit him.

"I bet I laid there and listened to you breathe for hours, I've never done that before." He said.

"What did Gabriel say to you? Was he mad?" I asked as we stood up to walk over to the girls.

"He wasn't, he actually said he didn't want me to make the same mistake he made, and he was happy for us, he actually pointed out how much I liked you before I realized it." He smiled as we walked hand in hand.

"The whole situation is a bit strange, but I won't try to understand it." I said.

"Don't." He said back. "I've never had a long distance relationship before but I want you to know I am going to do everything I can to make this work." He said.

All I could do was smile. The initial shock had worn off, I wasn't shaky anymore, but I still felt sick to my stomach.

"I'm going to do what I can to make this work." I said back repeating him.

"I told your dad about that left hook, he laughed." Spencer said.

"You told my dad about that?" I said with a frown then followed it with a smile.

"That was the highlight of my week. I have never seen some shit like that, I was so proud of you, I can't stand her. I can't count how many times I thought about paying someone to hit her." He laughed.

I held out my hand.

"$100 bucks please." I laughed.

"Wow, you aren't cheap are you?" He laughed back at me as he poked me in the side.

"I don't want your money." I smiled pushing his hand away.

He just smiled and we walked toward the girls.

"Time to go girls, we need to get home and do some laundry." I said grabbing Marie.

"We don't want to go home." Rayanne said running away from me.

"I'm serious, let's go." I said with my mom authority.

"Quite giving your mom the business." Spencer said as he laughed. "I get to see the different side of you." He smiled.

"It's ugly sometimes; I have to lay down the law." I smiled back squeezing Marie's hand.

Spencer helped each one of them into the car. He shut the door and as I opened the driver side door, he pushed it shut and pushed me up against the door. He put both hands on my face, and looked me deeply in the eyes.

"I really meant it when I told you I wanted you to move to California when you graduate, if that's too much for you to do, I will move here." He said, "Wherever you want to go, I want to be with you." He said as he opened my door.

All I could do was smile. That was the best gift he could ever give me. When we got back to my house, we watched some movies while the girls ran around the house. He didn't seem to mind. I did some laundry and we put in a kids movie. While the girls sat down to watch it, he helped me fold laundry.

They both wanted to sit next to him. They both wanted to climb on him. They both wanted to poke and pull at him. I was getting a bit annoyed and I knew I shouldn't but I didn't want to scare him off. They both started folding laundry. I just smiled because they never wanted to help fold laundry. Spencer showed them how to put it away while I made dinner.

After I put the girls in bed, which was another fight, Spencer and I sat down and had coffee at my kitchen table.

"Funny how things work out." I said smiling at him. I couldn't stop looking at him.

"I never imagined in my life that I would meet someone and they would cause me to feel the way I do." Spencer said staring at me. He never took his eyes off me.

"I never thought I would find someone I liked as much as Gabriel, and believe me; I am not comparing you to him. That's what made me realize how much I liked you, when I found myself not comparing you to him." I smiled at him.

"I really didn't follow you around, when I saw you, it really was just by the grace of God. I know that seemed creepy." He laughed.

"Yeah, it was, kind of hard not to think you were stalking me." I laughed back.

"Come here." Spencer said as he stood up and held out his hands.

He led me to the living room and we sat down on my couch. He wrapped his arm around me and kissed my forehead.

"This, this is what made me fall for you." He said taking a deep breath in.

I leaned on his chest and listened to his heart beat for hours. I still couldn't figure out what was wrong with him, but I stopped trying to. We didn't do anything that night, as a matter of fact, he stayed with me for three days and we didn't do anything but kiss. I took an extended vacation, my boss wasn't happy about it but I worked a bit from home. The next three days were spent doing things with the girls. It was weird to me because I had never had anyone around the girls, but it almost felt like he belonged there, in some strange way. We both knew he had to go back to Florida, and I dreaded it. I still felt like he wasn't going to come back, or call me again, or see me again. Maybe he was right; I did have a fear of being left.

I woke up for work that morning at 5:30, which was an hour earlier than I normally did out of the blue. Spencer was gone. He knew I was returning to work today and he left before I woke up. So many emotions came running to me than I didn't know what to feel. He left a note for me in the kitchen next to some beautiful roses and a small envelope. Inside the envelope was a check for $2000 and the note read:

"I knew that if we planned to be together when I left, I wouldn't want to leave, I knew that it would break my heart to have to leave. I did not want to see you upset. The last few days have been the best three days of my life, and I want you to hold onto those memories until I return. I did not sneak out on you, and I'm not going to let you go, I will call you as soon as I get back to my parents; I am going to stop and see Eli before I go home. I want you to take this money and buy yourself something Kensie, don't spend a penny of it on the girls. I didn't sleep last night, I watched you sleep and wondered what you were dreaming about. I began to miss you and I wasn't even gone yet. I will be back next month and we will see each other for as long as you want. Please don't cry, please don't be sad..."

I stood there and read and reread the words and was confused but I knew he was right. I wanted to text him to have a safe trip, but I didn't want to bug him. The money became obsolete; it was if it wasn't in front of me at all. I paid no attention to it. At the same time, I didn't want him to forget me; I guess I kind of figured that wouldn't happen. I sat in my kitchen drinking my coffee and began to collect every memory of him. I smiled and said out loud, *"God, please don't let me get hurt again."*

I went in to wake the girls up and Spencer had bought each of them a dozen roses, and left them an envelope that had $100 in it and told them it was their job to help do laundry and pick up their things. He told them he would miss them and that he would see them again soon. That just about broke my heart, I let someone get close to my girls and if he hurt me, it was going to devastate everyone.

He texted me that morning after I got to work, I finally realized he wasn't going anywhere. Everyone in my office was on me every second of the day about my trip and all they wanted to talk about was Gabriel. I didn't tell them anything bad, I just told them I had a great time. It occurred to me that I forgot to get an autograph from him for the receptionist. I promised I would do it as soon as I talked to him again. He emailed me that day, he asked me how things were going and I told him everything that had happened and he sent me back an email that told me he was truly happy that I could find something that made me as happy as I could be...and he was glad to be part of it. I felt better about the situation, and although somewhere deep inside me, I still loved him, and always would, I almost felt like I owed him more than I could ever give him.

Chapter 15-My Forever

Spencer and I continued to talk over the phone and via email for the next four weeks. After Gabriel came back from being out of the U.S., it made it difficult for me to talk to Spencer because they were pretty busy. He would shoot me a text from time to time, and I think it made my love for him stronger. I missed him horribly, but I kept plugging away doing what I had always been doing.

Four weeks had passed since I had seen him, and the girls bugged me every day asking when he was going to come back. He even talked to them a few times on the phone for a half hour each…that meant a lot to me. About two weeks later Gabriel and Spencer, along with the entourage, came down to meet my boss and our agency got to handle some of the business he needed for shooting. I felt good to be part of that, and he gave the receptionist her own autograph and she got a picture with him. They were going to be in Tennessee for about a week, I didn't see much of Gabriel except for at work, but Spencer made an effort to see me when he could.

On the third day of his arrival, I was sitting at my desk around 11:30 working on some things for Gabriel's movie and Rayanne walked into my office. I stood up with my heart pounding, freaking out that she was there by herself.

"What are you doing here baby? Is everything okay, are you with grandma?" I asked her as I held her hands and looked outside my office.

"Nope, Spencer mommy." She smiled at me.

A few minutes later Spencer walked in carrying Marie while talking to my receptionist. He was so damn sexy I wanted to eat him. He was holding my life in his hands.

"Hello…" He said as he bent down to kiss me.

The people in my office were looking into my office smiling; a couple of them casually walked by the door looking in.

"Hey you, what are you guys doing here?" I smiled back at him.

"I had your mom get the girls from day care and we decided to take you to lunch. I already checked with your receptionist and she said you didn't have any appointments." He laughed.

"I don't, I was working on some things for Gabriel but I can finish this afternoon." I said in awe.

After we had lunch, I had to get back to work. He kept the girls the rest of the day and took them to Nora's to go horseback riding. Luckily, Nora was there and the girls know how to ride. I missed the whole thing but Nora said it was the funniest thing ever and I was sorry I missed it. I wished he would have picked a day when I could have been there. I always thought him and I would go, not him go with my girls...but, it made me laugh hearing about how he really can't ride a horse.

Nora offered to keep the girls as Spencer was leaving and' she called me to ask if that was okay with me, and I said sure. Nora was always around my girls but they had only stayed with her a handful of times. They were excited because there was so much trouble they could get into on the ranch.

Spencer and I went out for dinner that night, did some sightseeing and I took him to the Grand Ole Opry. I could tell it was different for him, but he seemed to enjoy it. I was just glad he was there.

That night when we got back to my house, we sat on the couch and watched a movie; I fell asleep a half hour into it. He woke me up and led me into my bedroom. He began to kiss my neck, my face, my chest, but this time, he didn't stop himself. I rolled over on top of him and kissed his neck, his ear, his lips; I was in control of the situation now and wanted to be as close to him as I could be...

I slowly raised his shirt and kissed his stomach as he rubbed his hands all the way from my shoulders to my waist. His put his hands inside my shirt and lifted it off gently, he reached behind me to remove my bra and I began to get self-conscious. He didn't seem to mind what I thought about myself, or what I looked like under my clothes, he reassured me that I was beautiful and somehow I ended up on my stomach.

He started kissing my bare back and moved his way to my lower back. He was driving me nuts. He kissed me from my back to my feet and by this time it was 3 in the morning. I wasn't tired anymore, just wanted him so badly. I rolled over to my back and he took both my hands and put them above my head, his hands were clenched with mine, and I felt like we were one again.

He sat up above me and took his shirt off. I just admired how incredibly sexy he really was without his shirt on…for now, he was mine. I kept thinking about the mingling he had been doing back in California and how this time it was me laying there instead of someone else.

I hadn't been with anyone in about six months, there was this one time I slept with Clay after our divorce; it was a dumb moment where you just do what you think is right in the moment. I was so nervous, I was so scared. I felt like I was a virgin again and this was the first time I had even considered having sex with someone.

I reached down and unbuttoned his pants, but tried to refrain from touching him for some strange reason. I just didn't want to know what was in his pants until I felt it inside me…

He pulled down the shorts I had been wearing and then rubbed my panties and the sides of my legs, he kept kissing me and I felt like I was going to explode. He slowly lifted my backside up and pulled my panties down below my knees, my body started to ache. I started to tell him it had been awhile since I was with anyone but he put his finger on my lips and shushed me. As he slowly entered my body, every molecule inside me began to tremble. With every thrust and every moan, I felt like we were meant to be together. I watched his glossy eyes look deep into mine; he never took them off me. I do believe that was the longest I have ever had sex. I was out of breath but crying for more when we finally finished. He collapsed on the left side of me and I lay there speechless but still trying to catch my breath. It was like the world stopped for a short period of time and I was teleported to utopia. Maybe I just felt that way because I hadn't been with anyone in a while…Spencer was everything I could have ever asked for, he was passionate, loving, caring, and gentle; he was beautiful, even covered in sweat.

I know if it had been the past, I would have thought that just maybe he did all that to win, to win the game against Gabriel. To say he slept with me first, after all that had happened. I never even gave it a second thought after that.

He wrapped his long legs around my body and squeezed me almost to give me a laying down hug…but he didn't let go. Even after all of that and the sweet smell of sex in the air, I could still smell his cologne. He held me like I had never been held before. I was tired but wide awake. He kept his arms around me tight and eventually fell asleep. I listened to him breathe for what seemed like hours and held his arms around mine.

I soon realized that he was genuine, that there are guys out there that can be real. I was myself; I never had to try to make him happy. I never had to change myself just to keep him. I had been in relationships that I fought so hard to make that person happy, changing who I was because I didn't want to lose them at that time. I didn't have to do that with Spencer. It was natural; it was amazing; it was love although I never said it.

He would see me when he could for the next few days, I knew he was busy but we didn't have sex again that trip. The more and more I was around him, the more comfortable I got. When the movie was in post-production, Spencer came to stay with me for an entire month. Gabriel eventually found something else time consuming to do, then the movie was released and Spencer had to play PR. I didn't see him as often as I'd like to have, I didn't see him for a few months after that but we never stopped talking and emailing. I kept plugging away with school and never let it interfere with my daily life…I found myself less stressed and a lot more loved.

I wanted to tell him I loved him on several occasions. I did once, playfully, when he stopped in to see me unannounced, but I said it like I was saying it to my best friend. He just smiled at me.

Gabriel and I remained friends and emailed back and forth on occasion. I eventually came up with a great screen play idea and he pitched it to some people and a ghost writer wrote most of the manuscript. I felt good to have started part of that idea, once the manuscript was finished, Gabriel began filming it. I sang the main theme song to the movie but I refused to let him announce me as the singer. Spencer came up with a great fake name, and I never did it again. Being in a studio recording a song was very time consuming.

Spencer and I spent what time we could together, not seeing each other all the time really made it exciting when we were together. He ended up leaving Duggar with me, he never replaced Cairo, but he fit in nicely.

I never knew being with someone, sexually, mentally, and spiritually, could make you feel so complete. Spencer's mingling days were now over. It made me feel good when I logged on to my social network site one day, he had tagged me in a bunch of pictures and people were asking who I was. He replied by saying, 'my future.' I stopped trying to figure out what was wrong with him. He didn't put the toilet seat down, didn't put the toilet paper back on the holder, he always forgot to put the toothpaste away, he drank out of the milk container. I didn't mind because there was nothing else I could find that he did wrong. What was wrong with him was that he wasn't like everybody else, that's what was wrong with him, and he truly was my white knight.

He kept in great contact with me, and he always answered my calls. He never fell off the face of the earth, he wasn't married, he didn't try to buy my love, but he sure helped out when he was at my house and sent the girls and I gifts when he was out and about, he didn't take off to college, he was always on time, but he NEVER stopped opening my car door. Speaking of which, he gave his car to Josh, just gave it to him. He bought one with four seats.

I stopped searching for someone to love, stopped looking for people around me that might be 'the one' and I didn't cry every time I seen someone happy. Eventually we talked on the phone every day, and I saw him every chance he could get away. I know he spent mass money on plane tickets.

He ended up buying a four bedroom house outside of Santa Monica, he sent me a thousand pictures of every single inch of it, it wasn't as big as Gabriel's, but it was beautiful. When I graduated six months later, Spencer wanted to have a graduation party for me in California. My parents agreed to keep the girls for a few weeks while I went to Santa Monica. I put in my two week notice at the ad agency, knowing that I now had my journalism degree; I wanted to find a writing job.

I left on a Sunday, jobless, but this time, the plane flight was much different. I was with someone I truly loved; someone that made me feel what true love was…someone who never left me. When I arrived in Los Angeles, Liam picked me up. I just smiled and laughed to myself when I saw him.

"You don't even have to say anything." I smiled and said before he even said anything. He just smiled back.

When we finally got to Santa Monica, we pulled up in front of Spencer's house. There was tons of cars on the grass, driveway, people were everywhere. I was a bit confused. Spencer was standing outside the front door and smiled when he seen Liam pull up. He opened the door and gave me a huge hug.

"Are you having a party?" I asked him confused.

"Well yeah!" He said smiling back.

We went into the house and I was trying to actually look at the house around all the people. The kitchen was absolutely beautiful. Gabriel was there, as were a billion people I didn't know. Spencer's parents were there; they both gave me a hug and congratulated me. *Why were Spencer's parents there?*

"It's just a degree." I laughed.

"Oh, it's so much more than that." Blaine exclaimed.

"It's just a graduation party." I laughed.

I turned to my left and looked out the kitchen door, Spencer didn't send me pictures of the back yard; I never thought to ask about it. There were balloons everywhere and a pool! There was a pool...I was going to love staying here for two weeks without the girls! It was beautiful! I walked out of the door onto the patio and stared at the pool.

"For you, my dear." Spencer said appearing from nowhere as he put his arm around me and kissed my forehead.

"It's beautiful. I didn't know your house had a pool." I smiled back as I looked up at him.

I looked up and Nora was walking towards me. Nora was here too! *So why is Nora here?*

"I wanted your parents to be here but your mom was not letting the girls get on a plane. So, we are going to use a live feed to see them...just wait." Spencer said as he turned to say something to some body behind him.

"Nora! What are you doing here?" I smiled and hugged her tight.

"It took all I had not to tell you, not to fly with you, but I came in on a flight before you got here." She said laughing. "I'm so proud of you!" She smiled.

"Thank you, you have been my very truest and best friend, thank you for staying beside me all these years." I started to cry

"Your welcome honey, I don't mean to bring anything up, but I met Gabriel, and he is most definitely a hot ass. He doesn't stay in one place long, does he?" She laughed.

"I told you!" I exclaimed.

Spencer came out onto the deck with just about everyone following him that weren't already out there. He was carrying a lap top and my parents and girls were on the other side.

"Hey ladybug!" My dad exclaimed.

"Hi mom, dad, girls…" I smiled and said. Rayanne was trying to ask me something but my mom hushed her.

Spencer handed the lap top to Liam and Liam followed him over to me. Spencer grabbed two wines off of a plate someone was carrying behind him and handed one to me.

"Kensie, this party is part for your graduation, in which I am so proud of you for sticking out and part for the movie being produced that was started by you…each time we start production of a movie, we celebrate before we have to get busy filming. I never imagined in my life that someone very dear to me, Gabriel…" Spencer said as he held up his glass to Gabriel who was standing offside on the deck… "would be the reason I found something I was never really looking for, but it fell in my lap, and for that, I thank you my friend." Spencer said as they both took a sip of their wine.

I didn't know what to do, I wasn't sure if I should sip mine or not, so I did, a small sip. I was sort of standing there not really understanding what was going on. Spencer turned around and handed someone behind him his glass of wine.

"Now, we are also celebrating one other thing today, and I'm hoping it goes as I planned it to…" He said as he reached into his pocket. Spencer grabbed my hand and got on one knee and pulled out a box. *No, no, no, he isn't doing what I think he's doing is he?* My whole body began to shake and my eyes were huge.

"Kensie, I knew I was going to fall in love with you the first time I met you, I knew I wanted to be with you always the first time I touched you. There was something about you that made me feel like I have never felt, I always said I would never fall in love, never want to be in a serious relationship, but…I knew that was going to change the first day I met you. Kensie, I love you, will you marry me?" He said as he started shaking.

All I could do was stand there, I felt like everyone around me was spinning in a circle. I was dumbfounded, I never imagined he would tell me he loved me, let alone ask me to marry him. I just stood there. Stood there for my life; stood there like an idiot. Suddenly everything around me was on pause, I couldn't move. He just kept staring at me. I finally snapped back to this universe that I was in.

"Spencer, I never in my life imagined I would be standing here, let alone you standing in front of me, and I never imagined that anyone would ever make me as happy as I have ever been, you're almost too perfect to me; you've been so good to my girls, to me. To Gabriel…" I said as I lifted up my glass to him… "You are the reason I am here, you are the reason that I feel the way I feel now, all those years of holding on to my best friend; I owe this to you." I said as I smiled up at him. "I love you Spencer…" I said as I sat my wine down and got down on my knees and took both my hands to his face. "I knew I loved you for a long time, I always wanted to say it but didn't know how. I didn't know how to love anyone again until I met you. I LOVE you Spencer and I'd be honored to marry you." I said as I gave him a huge hug and squeezed him tight.

We both stood up and hugged each other, everyone started clapping and I looked up to Gabriel, but he was gone. I was too happy to worry too much about where he disappeared to. My makeup was running everywhere. I turned to the lap top and both my parents were crying. My girls were jumping up and down and yelling holding hands. I was dumbfounded and happy at the same time.

"I'm so glad that you said yes because I have something else to show you." He said as he grabbed the lap top. "I know we talked about this before and you told me if and when the time was right, you would stay so…I'm hoping you and the girls will come here to live, this is your house too now." Spencer said as we walked back into the house.

We went down a long hall way to a door. He went in first with the lap top and looked into the lap top.

"Rayanne, Marie, if your mom says yes, this is your room." He said as he scanned the room so they could see.

The room had two canopy beds in it, everything was pink and purple, dolls, Barbie's, boxes, ruffle curtains, dressers that were the same color, a table to draw and color on, anything and everything they could have ever wanted.

"How did you do this?" I said in awe.

"My mother, and Nora." He said as he looked behind me and Nora was standing there.

"You knew?" I looked at her and said.

"He emailed me a long time ago and told me of his plan, I told him everything he needed to know about the girls, what they liked and didn't, colors, toys, and his mom helped out with decorating." Nora turned around and Spencer's mom was standing there.

"Thank you; I don't know what to say to you all." I started to cry. Of course the girls were going ballistic and my dad was getting frustrated.

"The answer is yes." I said as I kissed his cheek.

I didn't see Gabriel any more in that two week period and it didn't seem to bother me; although I thought about him on occasion. I spent every minute enjoying that house. I was headed home an engaged girl and was quite happy about it.

I had fears of leaving my parents but over the next few months, the girls and I ended up moving to Santa Monica and I got a job for a newspaper. Gabriel suddenly became part of my everyday life, it wasn't weird at all, as a matter of fact, I stopped thinking about my past and him all together, however; that picture he gave me is still in the frame, sitting on top of my fireplace, the one that looks just like the one in Spencer's old apartment. Spencer continued to work for Gabriel but he also started doing some PR work for other people to lessen his load.

Chapter 16- Faith

Six months later, we decided to get married in Florida. I had already gone home to my parent's house to begin preparing for it. I stayed with them for two weeks. I didn't see Spencer at all during that time and we decided not to talk to each other. It was very hard not to call him. My mom and Nora helped out so much, they kept my sanity. Amanda flew in to help. I really enjoyed being around her. She was a very sweet person. One day I told her that I thought she should date Gabriel. She told me she didn't like him like that, they didn't get along real well some times and she told me she probably shouldn't tell me this, but she knew it wouldn't change how I felt about Spencer, but Gabriel told her he would never get over me. That touched my heart but I knew that my life with Gabriel would never be what I wanted it to be…it would never be what I had with Spencer.

Instead of Spencer having a suitable bachelor's party, he decided to drive to Florida, from California. I knew it was going to take days but he said he always wanted to do that and now was the perfect time to do it. I was concerned with that, since we agreed not to talk to each other before the wedding, and then I began to think maybe he had changed

his mind, or was ironing something out in his head which
bothered me. I guess I would live my life giving everything
a good analysis.

We all stayed at a hotel in Florida not far from the church
Spencer and I were getting married in. Amelia had rented a
beautiful place for us to have the reception. The night
before the wedding, Amanda and Nora, plus some girls I
knew from school and the ad agency all went out for drinks.
It was a very calm evening, and I so wanted everything to
be perfect. Mom and dad had the room next to me with the
girls. I went to bed relatively early because there was so
much that needed to be done.

I couldn't imagine the stress I was going to be under when
we started getting ready. The wedding was at 2; I got up at 9
and got in the shower. Amanda did my makeup and my
hair. She put huge ringlets all over and loosely piled them in
the back of my head. I decided not to use a veil, so we took
tiny little flowers that grew in the channel and she put them
all through my hair. The dress I had was made by a friend of
mine, she didn't charge me much, but it was an off white, it
was strapless, v-cut, it had smooth lines going down the
front of it, almost like creases but they were very subtle. It
came down to my knees and was longer in the back with a
train that had creases in it but it wasn't too long. I always
wanted a lacy wedding dress but since I had been married,
and although it was nothing like this, I no longer wanted the
lace.

My wedding colors were red and blue, and I was getting
nervous. It was 12 and we started getting the girls ready. As
I was putting flowers in Marie's hair, someone knocked on
the door…

"Everyone dressed?" Someone said as they slowly opened
the door. We all looked up and it was Gabriel. I jumped up
and ran over to him, giving him a huge hug. He stood there
and hugged me back for what felt like forever. That was the
first time since I hadn't seen him since I was 15 that he
clung to me so tightly for so long, and the feelings between
us were racing back and forth through our bodies.

"You look beautiful." He said and smiled.

"Thank you!" I said as I let go of his arms.

"He's here." Gabriel said and smiled.

"He's here, he's here…" I exclaimed as I turned around to everyone.

"He got here about an hour ago and I wanted to come and tell you that he IS here…" Gabriel said as he laughed, "…and to see if anyone needed anything." He finished.

"I don't think we do, I swore I wasn't coming out of this room until it was time to go." I laughed.

"Okay, well, then…I will see you soon." He said as he looked at me like he did the day I left Florida, like he did when we were kids, like he did when he loved me, but couldn't love me. I just stared at him until he shut the door. Neither of us smiled. I sat in my chair and began finishing Marie's hair. I just thought and thought and decided that we both knew that it just wasn't meant to be…Gabriel and me.

When it came time to walk down the aisle, I got so nervous I almost threw up. I hardly had any family left; I already knew what was going to happen. My side was going to be empty and everyone would be on Spencer's side. I would be sad no one was here to share it with me…my dream. My dad came in at quarter till 2 and got me. He gave me a hug and told me not to be nervous, grabbed my hand and said, "The wedding is going to be beautiful." I hadn't even been out yet to see what the church or the reception looked like when it all came together.

We began to walk down the hallway of the church and I could hear the music playing. I began to cry. The church was beautiful, there were red and blue flowers everywhere. We spent about $1000 on fresh flowers. As we turned to walk towards the pews, I could see everyone inside looking back at the doorway; it wasn't as empty as I thought it would be. My mother and Amelia were on one side sitting with each other, Blaine was on the other side seated next to Spencer's sister. All of my co-workers from the ad agency were there, including my old boss, no one really picked a side, but there were quite a few people there. I had a few aunts and uncles who showed up, and brought their children. Rayanne and Marie were standing next to Nora, and Amanda was my other bridesmaid. Spencer had Josh and Gabriel next to him.

Ah, my Spencer. I couldn't take my eyes off him, as he didn't take his eyes off me. He leaned over to say something to Gabriel. He had his hands crossed in front of him, smiling. He looked so beautiful standing there in his black suit; the sun was shining in the church windows. I began to cry so bad that I couldn't control it. As my dad walked me down the aisle, and squeezed my hand, I looked up at the windows of the church and blew my grandma a kiss in the air. Everyone was smiling and I cried harder. When I finally made it to the Alter-which felt like it took an hour to do; I just kept crying. The music stopped and Spencer was standing in front of me getting ready to recite his vowels. He reached over and wiped the tears from my eyes.

"Don't cry." He whispered as he smiled.

"I can't help it." I whispered back to him.

Spencer read his vowels to me and I started to say mine back but my voice was cracking and I couldn't quit crying. Everyone made an 'Awe' noise.

"I'm sorry." I said to everyone as I smiled and wiped the tears from my eyes.

I made it thru my vowels and the preacher announced us "Mr. and Mrs. Spencer Harrington. What an almost perfect feeling, to be married to my future, my Spencer, my life.

Everyone clapped and we walked down the aisle to the car outside the church.

"I didn't think you were going to make it through that." Spencer said smiling as we got into the car.

"I know, I'm so sorry, everything was so beautiful and there were more people here than I expected, and I…" I said as he put his index finger across my lips and shushed me.

"I told you, everything was going to be okay." He smiled back with his dimple and his beautiful green eyes.

The reception was amazing. My mom and Amelia did a wonderful job of putting everything together. As people started piling in, we sat down to eat. The food was wonderful; everyone kept hugging me and congratulating me. Gabriel came up and hugged me but it was short and he immediately let go of me to move on to Spencer.

Marie told me Ethan was cute and all I could think of was, *here we go again; the circle never ends.*

The wedding was almost perfect, until we realized that one of his cousins had knocked over the punch bowl and the girls had taken the figurine on top of the cake and put it back in upside down. There were finger prints all through the icing. All we could do was laugh. We cut it anyway.

Nora came up to me and hugged me tightly, smiling. Everyone was dancing and some of the family did karaoke. I couldn't keep my eyes off of Spencer, he amazed me. I didn't really say much, lost in my whole life of anxiety over if this would ever happen. Everyone really was…perfect. Spencer got up in front of everyone to make an announcement, I thought for sure he was going to make me get up and sing.

"For you Kensie, without this, I would have been lost." Spencer said as he raised his champagne to me and everyone took a drink of their champagne. He sat it down on the table in front of him and grabbed the microphone from the DJ.

What's he doing? I thought. Everyone was watching and I had never heard him sing before, only in the shower like he said, or in the car, especially in the car when we were driving, usually it was to classic rock. He really could play the piano, but I never heard him sing in front of anyone.

When the song came on I knew I had heard it before, but I couldn't remember what it was. I sat there in my dress, flowers in my hair. This was MY day, for once, a day made for me. My first wedding was never like this. All the mistakes I made led me to this, to this life, it was finally mine.

Everyone started clapping as he stood there waiting for his cue. Almost everyone was half drunk anyway, except me.

Even my dad was pretty wasted and he never drank. Everyone grew silent at once when Spencer began to sing.

'*When the road gets dark; and you can no longer see, just let my love through a spark; have a little faith in me. When the tears you cry, are all you can believe, just give these loving arms a try baby, and have a little faith in me, and have a little faith in me. Have a little faith in me*' Spencer was singing *John Hiatt*'s '*Have A Little Faith in Me.*' As he sang the song and didn't take his eyes off me, I looked over at Gabriel; he smiled and crossed his fingers on his chest in the form of a love symbol, then pointed at me. He really was part of my life for a grander design. I immediately began to cry. They were tears of joy, happiness, serenity, and peace. '*When your secret heart cannot speak so easily, come here darling...*' he continued to sing, '*I will catch your fall baby, just have a little faith in me...*' I wiped the tears from my eyes and he held out his hands to me. I got on the stage next to him and the DJ handed me another microphone. We both sang the rest of the song. I couldn't take my eyes off him. '*I've been loving you for such a long time girl, expecting nothing in return just for you to have a little faith in me...*' Everyone clapped when the song went off and we hugged each other for what seemed like forever. He put both hands on my face and kissed me. Everyone sighed and clapped.

"Gross." Marie said as she ran off with Ethan.

We flew out of Florida to Boston on our honeymoon, it was his favorite place and I had never been. My parents took the girls back to Tennessee for the next two weeks. I tried to convince him we needed to go to Paris, but I wasn't serious. He had a phobia about going on vacation out of the country for some reason. That was an unanswered question, almost like the many that we had in the past, but I didn't need answers anymore, I had him, forever. We spent a week in Boston and flew back to Tennessee to get Spencer's car. We drove back to California and that road trip was of the memories I will hold in my mind for eternity.

We stopped at places he had been along the way, places I wanted to see, it may have taken us a week to get back, but it was WELL worth it. Nora flew in with the girls not long after we got home and had taken a vacation to be in California for a few weeks. She pretty much stayed pool side the entire time.

I won't say it all went smoothly, it wasn't always perfect, but it was as close to perfection as I could have asked. I owed everything to my grandma. If it weren't for her allowing me to stay in Florida on my summer breaks, I would have never met Gabriel, in turn, I would have never met Spencer. For the first time in my life, my finances finally panned out. Although I didn't spend money lavishly, there wasn't a time that I didn't have what I needed.

Two years after we were married, my ex allowed Spencer to adopt the girls on the condition that they were allowed to call him any time they wanted. They kept calling and he stopped answering their calls, they finally stopped calling. They belonged to Spencer now and he was super protective of them.

I never thought it would happen, but last year I had our son, Xavier Blaine. He looks just like Spencer. He's beautiful in every way. I hope someday when he meets someone and takes them to the beach, that person appreciates him as much as I appreciated his dad.

Life becomes what you make it; no matter how crazy the dream, ironically enough, there is always a reason for chasing it.

About The Author

Mindy Sue Downs was born on August sixteenth, in Richmond, Indiana to Brenda and Ron Downs. She grew up with a younger sister, Ginger M. Downs. Mindy spent a lot of time writing and reading. After graduating in 1992 from Richmond High School, she put her college career on hold to have her three boys, Malachi, Gage, and Noah. The family moved to Hagerstown, Indiana in 2003. The small town lifestyle enabled her to focus on writing while working and taking care of her small children. Being a single mother was not an easy road but she managed to earn a Bachelor's Degree in Professional and Technical Writing from Indiana University East in 2013. Mindy currently ghostwrites, privately edits, and maintains two blogs.

Music Credits

'I want to know what love is'-Written and composed by Mick Jones and Lou Gramm, produced by Mick Jones and Alex Sadkin; performed by Foreigner from the 1984 *Agent Provocateur* album.

'Boardwalk Angel'-Written by John Cafferty, performed by John Cafferty and the Beaver Brown Band from the 1983 *Eddie and the Cruisers* soundtrack.

'Have a Little Faith In Me'-Written and performed by John Hiatt from the 1987 *Bring the Family* album.

'Total Eclipse of the Heart'-Written and produced by Jim Steinman, performed by Bonnie Tyler from the 1983 *Faster Than the Speed of Night* album.

'Big Girls Don't Cry'-Written by Fergie and Toby Gad, performed by Fergie from the 2006 *The Dutchess* album.

'I Will Remember You'-Written by Sarah McLachlan, Seamus Egan, and Dave Merenda, produced by Pierre Marchland; performed Sarah McLachlan from the 1999 *Mirrorball* album.

Picture and Cover Credits

Sandra Strange-Strange Photography-Author Photo

WWW.ThinkStockPhotos.com-Cover Photo

Made in the USA
Lexington, KY
13 May 2018